FITNESS FREEDOM

FINDING HEALTH AND SELF WHILE INCARCERATED

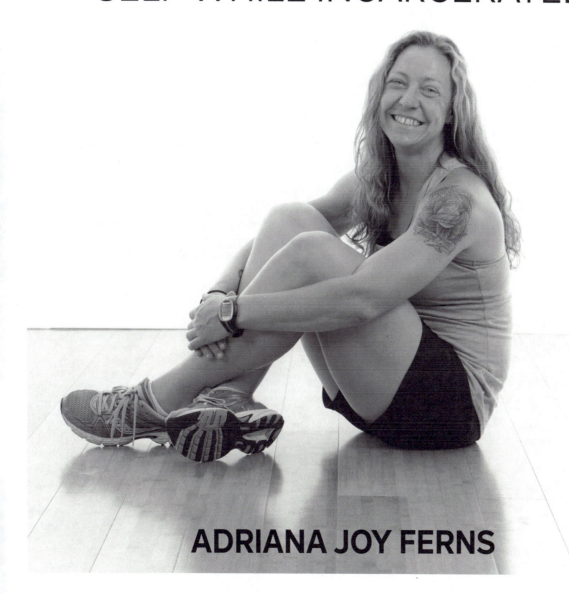

ADRIANA JOY FERNS

FITNESS TO FREEDOM

FINDING HEALTH AND SELF WHILE INCARCERATED

WRITTEN BY: ADRIANA JOY FERNS

Copyright August 25, 2017

TXu 2-057-211

Time

"As the calendars flip, I sit and now I finally see how precious time is. Someone once said, use your time wisely. I neglected to do so and now I'm looking at time. Time to reflect, time to change, time to realize what one bad choice can take away…my free time. All I have now is time. Time to think about when I was free, what freedom really means and what it is to cherish my time. Now that I can truly see how time flies, I promise God I will use every second, minute and hour as if it were my last. If I can be forgiven this time, yet another time. For all the times I've said this before, this is the last time. For the rest of my time on this earth, I promise to try and do right, I just need some time."

From the Journal of Adriana Joy Ferns 2008
Essex County Jail

ABOUT THE BOOK

With so many books out there written by and for men on the topic of health and fitness, few speak to the unique experiences and challenges of women living in the prison system. In Fitness to Freedom: Finding Health and Self While Incarcerated, Adriana shares both her lessons learned and the fitness and nutritional program that helped her and other women—especially those who are incarcerated and want to overcome the obstacles standing between their realities and the most hopeful visions and dreams they hold for their lives. Adriana's methods work because they were born of her own experiences as a woman incarcerated, providing her the knowledge, hope and viable fitness strategies specifically for incarcerated women.

Rooted in the lessons and experiences from her own life and first drafted on napkins and scraps of paper from Adriana's prison cell, Fitness to Freedom: Finding Health and Self While Incarcerated provides structured workouts that will work in county segregations, halfway houses and federal fitness centers, as well as eating plans and recipes that will work even for people restricted to food from commissary dining halls. Peppering her personal story with the workouts and recipes that made her successful today, Adriana is an inspiration to other women seeking healthy and happy lives, no matter where they began or on what road they may find themselves now.

CONTRIBUTIONS

EDITOR: KAITLIN MURPHY

BOOK DESIGN BY: ERIC SCHALL

ACKNOWLEDGMENTS

I began this book on Sunday, June 13, 2010, writing on napkins while being held in Wyatt Federal Detention facility in Central Falls, Rhode Island. I did not know it at the time, but I still had so much growth to do, and there were so many who would help me along the way.

I want to start by thanking God and everyone who had faith in me along the way, including: my mother Mary-Lou Ferns; my brother John Daniel Capaldi Ferns, for supporting me despite all my mistakes and lessons; my neighbors Jon and Kathy Lussier for putting up with me despite my problems and bad behavior; and my cousin Rachel Goldberg for typing and doing the first edit from a bunch of scraps of paper.

I would also like to thank my invaluable friends, including Cindy and Cory Milone and Rhodes Pierre for sticking by me and always believing in my visions; Laura Jenkins, the sister I never had that was the start of my walls breaking down; Laura Giannotti one of the warmest, kindest people I'm blessed to know; and "MY TRIPOD" Cortney Lancaster, one of the most caring people I've ever met who took me in when things got rough, always treated me like one of the family and guided me to my therapist, Brandi Gifford, who helped me through my father's sickness and death and taught me to trust and open myself up again. Brandi; you made me know I can do anything despite my learning issue and helped me to see my strengths and believe in myself. Camilla, thank you for all your faith in me and wise words. Darrell Dillon, my brother from another mother and training partner. Stevie V for always being able to cheer me up. My girlfriend Cindy Chadderton who was dropped from the sky and into my life, your support means the world! I'd also like to thank my Probation officer Clara King who showed faith in me despite all the people she must deal with who don't stay on track.

Stephen Ouellette, thank you for being one of the biggest support systems when I was on the inside, and on my transition out. For all of my other friends and family I didn't mention, I love you all and appreciate everything you have done for me. Without your faith in me I would not have grown into who I am today.

DEDICATION

This is dedicated to my father, John Ferns, who passed on November 10, 2012. I love you, Daddy!

PREFACE

As many incarcerated women do when they are ready to turn their lives around, when I was incarcerated in March of 2007 I turned for help to self-help books. I read everything I could get my hands on, from The New World of Self- Healing by Bente Hansen and The Power of Karma by Mary T. Browne to books on various religious practices that had helped other people. Yet somehow, even with all the books out there on reinvention, it wasn't easy to find books that could speak directly to what I was facing.

First, while there were many how-to workout books to choose from, I could not find an exercise and eating plan that fully accommodated the realities of food served in prison. Second, most of the books reflected men's experiences in prison, not women's. The hole in the literature did make sense. After all, men represent a much higher proportion of the prison population, and there is little that combines what works in health and fitness with an experiential knowledge of women's lives in prison. It's not just the literature that provides less support for women. Monitor on Psychology reports that "in most jurisdictions, women are offered fewer programs than men," and it may be that the disparity is taking its toll. According to Dr. Stephanie Covington, co-director of the Center for Gender and Justice in La Jolla, California, "[I]n the last 10 years, the male prison population has increased 45 percent, while that of women is up 81 percent." i When a greater percentage of women have mental health and substance abuse problems (incarcerated or not), it is absolutely essential that physical health be better addressed. Dr. Covington's recommendations focus on increased therapeutic treatment for trauma and greater contact with inmates' families, and as a former substance abuser and current trainer, I believe that physical fitness and health is a key part of the treatment that is lacking in women's prisons today.

As is true for many incarcerated women, I did not just need a tool book, recipe book or memoir. I wanted something that spoke directly to me in the voice of someone who had found her way through the challenges to physical and emotional health, as well as professional fulfillment and success. I needed story and strategy combined, something that spoke to my experiences as a woman in prison while providing a practical plan for how to create a healthy life when I'd had no model to illustrate that for myself.

Over time and through trial and error, I created the program that worked for me and wrote the book that I had needed at the time. It has been an arduous process to find the health that came from my own mistakes and experiences in prison, and despite the success I am grateful to be enjoying now, I continue to heal from the pain that led to my failings and the pain I caused for others as a result of them.

I wrote this for the women who need the same thing I needed in my own prison cell over five years ago. If this book can provide even one of you the tools and story you need to hear, it will be worth every effort, every word.

TABLE OF CONTENTS

Part I - My Story

Chapter 1 - Girl Meets the System 3

Chapter 2 - Detox: Changing My Mind 5

Chapter 3 - Prison: The Weight Gain 6

Chapter 4 - Taking off the Pounds in Prison 8

Chapter 5 - Beyond Fitness: Finding a Vocation 13

Chapter 6 - Halfway House to Home Confinement: Making the Transition 19

Chapter 7 - Dealing With Setbacks (Even Big Ones) 22

Chapter 8 - Relationships (Ugh…) 25

Chapter 9 - Ah, so that's why detours happen:
                Writing a Book and Becoming a Better Trainer at Wyatt
                Detention Facility 2

Part II - Your Turn

Chapter 10 - Time for a Pep Talk 33

Chapter 11 - Creating an Exercise Routine That Works in Prison 39

Chapter 12 - Planning a Diet that Fuels You 49

Chapter 13 - Recipes That Work Behind Bars 61

Chapter 14 - Staying Motivated 67

Chapter 15 - Workouts in Detail: Beginner to Advanced 73

Part III - Afterword

Notes 101

Appendix

Glossary of Exercises 104

Glossary of Equipment 106

Visual Demonstrations of Exercises 107

PART I
MY STORY

CHAPTER 1

GIRL MEETS THE SYSTEM

When I was ten years old my family moved from Providence, Rhode Island to the quiet suburb of Coventry. Though I wasn't an outcast and was dubbed social, I never felt I fit in. I did not have any real connections or fall in with any particular group of friends. I struggled in school and nobody could figure out why I couldn't seem to understand what was being taught. Every year when I got my new notebooks and school supplies, I thought to myself, "I'm going to be smart this year." But with every embarrassment at what I didn't know, I withdrew a little more from the people who were trying to help. My parents told me I just needed to try harder, but I only alienated myself further as the material became more complex. While my parents were generally good to me, nobody knew how isolated I felt because I hid it well.

By the time I was fourteen, I had become disruptive at school and spent most of my after-school time in detention. While in and out of counseling and well into my high-school education, at thirteen I was diagnosed with ADHD. I was put on various medications including Ritalin, Desiprimime, Welbutrin, Prozac and Zoloft. I hated the medication and how it made me feel, and when I was told by the therapist that I needed Ritalin, I overdosed in order to make them take it from me. I ended up in the hospital, was questioned by more counselors and was diagnosed with depression. When I was fifteen, I began experimenting with weed until I was high almost every day. I ran away from home numerous times, joined a gang and smoked and sold pot, basically showing no regard for anyone, including myself. My parents tried everything, but I just felt lost and continued to behave badly. One day, they just gave up. They told me they could no longer deal with me and my actions and that I had to leave the house. I felt I was a lost cause in every way. I was taken to family court and issued Ward to the State by the judge. I spent my sixteenth birthday in a group home being assessed. I made my way through the questioning by manipulating, persuading counselors and psychologists that I was fine, just a little misunderstood. It worked. I was released back to my parents' custody after a few weeks of assessment.

After high school, my parents told me I had to take a college class and earn at least a B for them to pay for it. While I continued to smoke pot daily throughout my psychology class, I was surprised to love it and earned an A. But I resisted when my parents insisted I go full-time. As I saw it, if school had shown me anything in most of my time there, it was that I was not smart enough to handle college full-time.

So without telling my parents, I dropped everything but writing. When they thought I was in school, I was skipping class to get high with my friends. And when my parents eventually found out, I never went back.

By the time I was nineteen, pot and other psychedelics had led to cocaine. I was into the rave scene and spent my time working on weekdays and from Friday after work to Sunday night, partying with no sleep. I was in and out of unhealthy relationships, constantly putting myself in situations that could have gotten me killed. I lived like this for fourteen years.

When I was twetnythree, my then-boyfriend had a sister whose boyfriend was a dealer. He said he'd pay me and give me free weed just to help him transport pot from Arizona to Rhode Island. I lived my life getting high, partying and blacking out regularly. Though I had not yet hit the bottom, I did not care whether I lived or died.

By 2006, I was living in a small apartment in Providence, and an acquaintance said he had a great deal for me. All I had to do was drive some meth to New Jersey. I was a cocaine addict and did not like meth so I figured it would be a great way to make money and stop getting high eventually. After being awake for two or three days on cocaine, I decided to take the chance. It was a lot of money, and I was told I could make at least $100,000. I was either going to get rich or go to prison.

Well, I didn't get rich. One of the guys involved had been caught doing a deal in another state, and I had put myself right in the middle of the set-up to catch him. I was arrested by the DEA and FBI on March 3, 2007 and held without bail in Passaic County. While waiting for my trial, I lived in Passaic County Jail.

CHAPTER 2

DETOX: CHANGING MY MIND

There is no medication given to help cocaine addicts detox. You come off it cold turkey, and most addicts can remember the painful process clearly. Somehow I did not have withdrawals. Maybe I was in shock? I felt immense relief a few days after being caught. Finally, I could be done with living this way. My mind became clear enough to realize that if I did not change, I was going to die. I'm still not sure how, but somehow clarity landed on me, and I wanted to stay alive. As I saw it, there was no way I should have stayed alive after the abuse I had inflicted on my body, and I decided I was still here to fulfill some purpose. I made a promise to myself that I would spend the time I was about to serve becoming better than I was when I had been arrested. I would make something of myself. I knew I needed to stop wasting my life and figure out how.

CHAPTER 3

PRISON: THE WEIGHT GAIN

Unfortunately, the mere decision to improve did not result in an immediate healthy outlook or life. It doesn't work that way. When I came off drugs, I turned to food. While that is common for recovering addicts, it is even tougher to avoid in prison, where other than mail, food is the focal point of a prisoner's day. Also, with food contracts for prisons often going to the lowest bidder, most of the food is what is cheapest: junk food. Food trays in prison are better in some facilities than in others, but for the most part they continue to be terrible, full of cake, cookies and white bread with almost every meal. Women who want to become healthy in prison have to learn to eat well without the option of visiting the local supermarket to select the quinoa, heart-healthy steel cut oats, olive oil replacements, or any farm fresh foods that other diet books advise. Also, contrary to what many people think about prison from the movies—places full of well-equipped gyms where everyone works out (which may be closer to reality in male facilities but is still exaggerated)—many women do not have regular access to the equipment we need to take care of our bodies. Women from all over the country have shared experiences with me that ring true with my own, painting a grim picture of diet and fitness and revealing a unique set of challenges I believe prison systems have to do better to address. However, incarcerated women can't exactly hold their breath waiting for the right supports to get moving and eating right. As I cited earlier, in most jurisdictions women are offered fewer programs than men and the services provided reflect little recognition of the traumatic paths that led them into the criminal justice system in the first place.

The facility in Passaic County where I lived was on the low end of the spectrum. In winter, we had no heat or hot water for two months. To shower, we used a bucket and the hot water spigot used for coffee. We would mix cold water from the shower with the boiled water, dip a cup in and pour it on ourselves to wash up. When the men's facility above us had a leak in the toilet system, the brownish-yellow water leaked through our ceiling onto a young woman's bed while she was asleep, making her sick for two weeks.

In approximately three months of being locked in a room about 24-24 square feet, I gained thirty pounds. The uptick on the scale continued in the year I awaited trial while working in laundry and volunteering for a program speaking to city kids about poor choices and peer pressure.

I gained the weight because I spent most of my time eating, reading and watching TV in a twenty-three-hour lockdown cell in a small dorm with thirteen other women. If we had recreation time on a particular day, we had three options. The first was in a dirty indoor recreation room, which was about thirty to thirty-five feet long by 15 feet wide and housed a few pull-up bars. As second and third options, there were two gyms on the roof, out in the fresh air with a volleyball net and two basketball hoops. Unfortunately, we rarely were allowed to use the open air gyms (three times a month at most). When we asked, we were told the men were using it. We did have use of a smaller indoor room five or six days per week, but at the time I was not motivated to do more than eat and sit around. The commissary offered pizza, and once a week I would eat almost a whole pizza by myself. I started as a laundry worker for the floor so I would get extra trays of food. Then I became a food worker, which gave me access to extra trays of food and the microwave. I would cook giant meals with Ramen noodles and tray food: processed cheese and meats, mayo, ketchup, white rice in trash bags for the whole dorm. I know. Ugh. If you are incarcerated and eating similar food, please, stop!

Growing up, I had always been fit. I was hyperactive, playing sports whenever I could. Even in my addiction, I danced regularly around my house, in clubs and anywhere I felt I could get away with it. I also hit the gym on and off. So when I saw the scale tick upward past a thirty-pound gain, I was disgusted with myself. How had I had let myself get to this point?

One afternoon, soon before being transferred to a facility in Newark, I told the chubby reflection that looked back at me in the mirror, "That's it! I'm fat! I'm getting in shape!" I didn't care what the obstacles were, or how strange it would feel being surrounded by people who were not doing the same thing. I would figure out a plan that could work in prison.

When I began, it was about me. I had no idea it would work well enough to share, or that by the end, it would be about you.

CHAPTER 4

TAKING OFF THE POUNDS IN PRISON

In 2008, some inmates filed a Class Action Complaint against the Passaic County Jail for inhumane living conditions and violation of constitutional rights. During this time the federal male and female inmates, myself included, were moved to the Essex County Facility in Newark, New Jersey. There, after committing to losing 30 pounds, I spent the free time I had running up and down the stairs in the pod, the living space that houses inmates. I also did exercises I could do with my body alone: push-ups, sit-ups, tricep dips, everything I could think of. I was the only one doing it and at first, other women made fun of me. But eventually they began to join me. The food was a little better than it had been in Passaic County, offering more vegetables and fresh fruits. But it was still pretty bad, and I began doing research on prison food and discovered why. The Daily cost to feed a prisoner in Florida was only $2.32 and the cost for a prisoner in California was $2.45. The Daily cost to feed the average American was $8.12. That's a big difference between prisoners and free citizens.[ii]

So I got a job in the cafeteria and figured out how to combine different food choices to eat better than I had been in the previous facility. At the same time, I was getting little clues about what I might be good at on the outside. Earlier I mentioned that in Passaic County I had volunteered in a program working with teens. It was called the Reality Check program, and in addition I had begun teaching a Ghanaian woman to read and write. Though the program was not available in Newark after the move from Passaic, I continued to work with her in the new setting anyway, adding one Korean woman and a few Latina women (one who taught me some Spanish in return) to my "class." It turned out that fitness wasn't the only thing that interested me. Watching them progress, I found that I loved and took great pride in teaching.

Of course, there had been emotional problems for me that had led to my rebellion and drug use, and at some point I would have to confront those problems. They had been deep enough to keep me from turning my life around in the past and I wouldn't be able to ignore them forever. But for me, gaining physical health and discovering a sense of purpose had to come first. It would create the jumping-off point for the even harder changes I would have to make later.

I wondered, could the same be true for other women? When we don't yet know how to handle the emotional wounds that threaten to derail us every day, can we at least begin to regain control over our health and find courage and purpose through fitness and exercise? For me, the answer was yes. Fitness was the window through which I could see and reach toward whatever was beyond the small, constricting world I had occupied for too many years.

Finally, on October 2, 2008, I went to trial. After one hour of testimony and rebuttal, I was convicted of conspiracy to possess with the intent to distribute methamphetamine. I was sentenced to three years in prison followed by five years of probation, and the year and a half I had spent in the two county facilities were applied toward that time. That meant I had a year and a half to go.

Below are a few things I learned in Essex County that you might try starting for yourself.

In the Newark facility in Essex County, I improved my diet. I knew about the strategy of eating well that focused on multiple small meals per day, and I began my diet change with switching to five to six small meals per day. It looked something like this:

Daily Meal Intake

Breakfast: Plain oatmeal or grits with real fruit juice and/or milk

Snack: Cereal bar and one piece of fruit

Lunch: Meat, vegetable and one complex carbohydrate (rice, pasta, potato)

Snack: Nuts and fruit, cereal or Carnation shake (almost every facility sells these in the commissary with the exception of fruit)

Dinner: Meat and double veggie or meat, veggie and 1 complex carbohydrate (rice, pasta, potato). Replace white with wheat options when possible.

Diet helped speed up my weight loss, but I also had to become active. Depending on how your facility is set up, you can use what you have in almost any circumstance (even solitary!). For me, my activity on a normal day in Essex County looked like this:

> **First Exercises**
>
> - Jogging up the stairs, around a tier and back down, 5 – 10x
> - Jogging up the stairs walking lunges around the tire, jog back down
> - 3 sets of 10 push-ups (adding reps as I got stronger)
> - 3 sets of 25 body weight squats
> - 3 sets of 20 tricep dips
> - Various ab exercises including crunches, sit-ups and planks
>
> Take about 10 minutes to do some basic stretches before and after your exercises.

I had played soccer when I was younger, and I added it to my routine when I found a volleyball to kick off the gym wall. This was a great cardio workout, and eventually the recreation director gave me a real soccer ball. I was thrilled. Seven days per week I stuck to my little self-made workout, weighing myself every week. In three months I lost fifteen pounds. Encouraged by the results, I started running the stairs and playing off-the-wall soccer right after breakfast on top of my nighttime routine. After I served and ate breakfast in my new job in the kitchen, I did one cardio exercise for as long as I had, usually thirty minutes or so. After dinner I continued with my old routine.

Being locked up is hard enough in itself, but trying to eat right and exercise in a county or lock can take all you've got. Some days it was hard to get out of bed. Things still were far from perfect, but exercise helped to pass the time, and when you are incarcerated that is reason enough to start. My spirits rose and I did not feel so down about the reality of my life, and by the time I was sentenced and on my way to federal prison, I had lost about twenty pounds and had defined my muscles.

After six months in Essex County, pleased with my results and ready to strive for more, I was moved to Danbury Federal Prison in Danbury, Connecticut.

This facility was exactly what it sounds like: a camp for adults. It was minimum security and there were no fences, gates or locks on any of the doors or windows. You could walk away at night if you really wanted to. I think the reason no one ever did is because most people in this facility only had a few years to go and an escape charge would be much worse. Compared to the previous places where I'd stayed, it felt more like a college dorm. It was even on a campus that included a gym in a separate building, down a huge hill in back of the facility. There was an outdoor track, and a cafeteria with much healthier food choices in the cafeteria and the commissary.

There were around 200 women in the camp, and we were housed all in one building. We had a salad bar and always had a choice of meat, soy, pancakes or plain oatmeal. We had a variety of cereals to choose from, with low-fat or skim milk for breakfast, and we were given fruit twice a day. Anyone who is or has been incarcerated knows commissary food is for the most part garbage, but in Danbury at least it was better than it had been at my previous facilities.

There was a one-quarter mile track and an indoor gym with stair steppers, a spin bike, a recumbent, a fan bike, a treadmill, and an elliptical trainer. There were free weights and some Nautilus and cable equipment. Motivated by my progress and weight loss, I was ready to finish it off.

The next box shows a sample of how I handled my eating in the camp. The tips will be especially helpful for those in Danbury or a similar facility, but regardless of where you are, try a close adaptation.

Menus

Breakfast: 1 can of 100 percent orange/pineapple juice, plain oatmeal or cream of wheat, glass of milk. 32 oz. or other water jug to carry throughout your day/job.

Pre-lunch snack: Granola bar from commissary (check sugar count; high in protein, lower in sugar).

Lunch: Lots of veggies from the salad bar. Romaine or spinach for lettuce (rather than iceberg) if available. If not, pile on the fresh veggies. Small amount (no more than 1 TBSP) of vinaigrette dressing. Heart-healthy meat, sometimes soy and a bread, pasta, rice, or potato (I only ate wheat bread or baked potatoes. I never used butter or salt to season my food). Choose baked over fried whenever possible. Water with lunch, before, during and after.

Pre-dinner snack: granola bar, fruit.

Dinner: Similar to lunch. Use the salad bar if you have one and whatever veggies are available.

They provided amazing looking desserts at Danbury, but I usually declined. If you have trouble coming off of sugar, try to replace it with fruit or yogurt to start, and you'll get there. (Confession: Every two weeks or so, I would get a sweet potato pie and a sweet tea with lunch. After lunch I usually had coffee. I used to put vanilla cappuccino, cream, and sugar in it for my sweet of the day. We do need some small pleasures!)

Once I had access to the better facility at Danbury, I kicked up my workout routine. After dinner six nights a week, I would hit the gym for two hours straight. If you can manage only part of that, start with every other day. Once you get a routine going six days per week, you can alternate light with heavy days and alternate cardio with weights and abs.

After my nighttime workouts, I would have a Carnation instant breakfast from the commissary (where I was there were no protein shake options but you may have them in your facility), go to bed around 9:30 pm and sleep like a baby. Whether you are wrestling with your demons or just getting into shape, there is nothing like a good workout to squeeze out the tension and allow you to sleep—even in an uncomfortable cell and bed, far from home.

Finally, when you are doing tough workouts all week, it is important to take a day off. On my day off every week, I started doing yoga. Nobody was helping me and I had to push myself when I didn't want to do anything at all. If you need support, look for a workout partner to motivate you. I also read fitness books and magazines for tips. With the exception of a cold and a few bad period days, I stayed on my workouts consistently for my whole six months at the camp. My body fat went from 22% to 19.1% during the time I was there, and I dropped five more pounds. Yes!

As my fitness and health improved, mental health began to follow. For the first time in a long while, I felt happier, stronger and more hopeful.

As other women saw my results, they began to approach me for advice and guidance. It was the first time I saw that bettering myself could have a positive impact on others, inspiring them to do the same. It felt like...a life. I had never thought of myself as a motivator. I had done my own thing regardless of what others said or did. But here I was, motivating other women who needed the same things I needed. In prison, as my skills presented themselves to me through the work I was doing, a new plan started to form for what I wanted to do with my life on the outside.

CHAPTER 5

BEYOND FITNESS: FINDING A VOCATION

Your life is not on hold while you are incarcerated. Fitness may open the door for you, but you can use this time to figure out what you want to do on the outside. It may only be an itch in your heart right now and you can't put your finger on what you want. That's fine if you are trying different things that could translate to a profession when you get out. If you already have a sense of what your dreams and talents are, start figuring out which skills you need to gain in order to apply those talents and achieve your goals when you get out. How can you gain those skills now?

Use right now to figure out who you are and what you want to do. Then start getting there. I know this may be harder than it sounds. In this chapter I will share how it happened for me, so take what is helpful and leave what is not.

As a recovering addict, I was required to complete a drug program while incarcerated. They offered a forty-hour program in the camp but I knew it would not be enough to help me. So instead of taking the easy way out as I had always done in the past, I admitted myself to a more extensive, nine-month program in the Danbury FCI, a maximum security facility down the hill from the camp in Danbury. It was a five-hundred-hour live-in program with about fifty other women, and its leaders emphasized seeing ourselves as a community of women all trying to rehabilitate.

There, the rules were even stricter than they were in the rest of the compound. I attended community group once per day, group therapy three times per week and regular instruction about criminal thinking errors and attitudes. I truly wanted to become a better person, so I listened to these errors and attitudes and looked at myself to see where I was going wrong. I realized that just as most people do when making poor choices, I had been feeling sorry for myself and blaming others for mistakes I clearly had chosen to make. This realization was key in kick-starting my emotional growth and self-esteem. I saw that I wasn't just a "bad person" or "dumb." When I had felt misunderstood and confused (as everyone does at some point) instead of reaching out for help I had become self-destructive. The more I applied the new tools I was learning, the faster I grew and the better I felt about all aspects of my life. There were optional groups also, including the health and wellness class I picked, along with diversity groups and a group that kept the community unit clean.

The quality of the food behind the fence at Danbury was as high as it had been at the camp, with an even bigger salad bar. I would pile my plate full of spinach, mixed greens, a variety of vegetables, beans and chicken or whatever other meat was offered. There was also a large selection of cheeses and fruits like melons, apples, oranges and more. People often left their fruit behind, and knowing the uneaten fruit would be thrown away, I took it for a snack later.

There was a giant track outside the commissary as well as racquetball and basketball courts. Inside there was a gymnasium, a cardio area and a weight room. As is true in any facility, there were things we complained about. While there were three treadmills, two elliptical machines, one stand up machine, two recumbent bikes and two spin bikes, there was not nearly enough equipment for more than one thousand five hundred women. Plus, we were only allowed to sign up for one machine for thirty minutes and there was always something broken. But when I shifted my mindset to see the possibilities instead (try it a few times and it gets easier), I realized that this facility did have more weights than the camp had. There were step aerobics classes four nights per week, and an aerobics class as well as yoga on the weekends. It took a while for me to find the right routine, and I had to learn to dismiss the drawbacks and be creative with what I had. I suggest you try this too.

After noticing all the work I was doing, the athletic director at the camp recommended that I ask the director of recreation about teaching a class. The only available position available was custodian, and I took it after hearing that I could use the facilities as much as I wanted when the work day was done. What I was doing caught on at this facility as it had previously, and women started to approach me during my abdominal exercises to ask if they could join me. So many joined that one of the correctional officers who worked in recreation said I was taking up too much room in the gym and I needed to run a class. I was ecstatic!

I studied for and passed a test in fitness instruction. I started an abs class, and with the help of a girlfriend we'll call Jessie, I ran a circuit training class, creating different stations where inmates spent sixty seconds on each before circulating to the next. The class became popular and I had to create a sign-up sheet limiting it to a manageable number of spots.

A new picture started to form of my life after incarceration, and every day it became clearer. Earlier I had learned I loved teaching another inmate how to read, but by now I had figured out it was fitness I wanted to teach. People responded to the classes and succeeded in meeting and maintaining their fitness goals. They enjoyed my workouts and I loved seeing that I could bring laughter and fun to such a dismal daily life. As the days passed, more women wanted in and people urged me to start another class, so I cleared it with my boss and worked with the department head on a schedule. This was also when I set my fitness and life goals for myself and encouraged others to do the same for themselves. My earlier goals were general, but for the first time I had them, and I kept them in plain view where I would see them often. I suggest you do the same, although knowing what I know now, I also recommend breaking them down into short-term goals that will lead to the larger goals, as well as activities you can do daily or weekly in order to get there. Then, you can create a weekly and daily inventory to track your progress.

Fitness Goals

- Run more than 5 miles.
- Improve balance.
- Build strength.
- Improve cardiovascular endurance.
- Reach the best physical condition I have ever achieved.

Life Goals

- Use my learning experiences as tools for learning, not fuel for regret.
- Stay consistent in exercise and eating routines.
- Enter into a field because I enjoy it, not just for money.
- Focus on my inner issues and do the work to heal them.
- Change the attitudes that don't benefit me.

Weekly Inventory

- Create a weekly inventory aligned to end goals and important dates. Is it the date of a hearing? A birthday or your child's birthday? The date of an upcoming visit? The date you get out? If you're in for life, mark dates you can look forward to.
- Consider what makes you proud. As you add to your weekly inventory, what can you do now and when you return home that can contribute in a way that will continue to make you proud?

> ### Daily Inventory
> - Every night, list what you accomplished and what you want to accomplish tomorrow.
> - What opportunities are there for pushing yourself a bit further and adding to your list?

On the night for sign-ups for my new class, the entire hallway was packed with women wanting to join. I was floored. They were screaming and pushing, and an officer actually had to come and take me off the sign-ups—it was almost a damn riot! The class was overcrowded, leaving the length of the gym to the volleyball floor packed with moving bodies. By the second week, the few people who were not serious dropped out, making the class more manageable to lead. Word spread throughout the prison and I asked the recreation director for some new equipment. To my surprise, she handed me some catalogs and told me to pick out a few things. She ordered more medicine balls and a holding rack for weights. I found mats and Pilates balls that had been stored, and I was able to supply my classes with a diverse set of workouts that would keep challenging them.

Eventually, a few of my peers from class suggested I get the whole gym. The officers eventually gave me two evenings per week of a full gym, splitting it with open volleyball. I decided to push it one more step and asked my work supervisor if this could be my new job. I was thrilled when he and the recreation supervisor both approved it, with the caveat that I add a morning class. That day I officially became an abs instructor for the facility, or to my classes "Abs Lady."

What I learned from this is that sometimes all you have to do is ask. You will need to be prepared with a plan, whether they say yes immediately or you are challenged. But it is a good practice for when you get back into a society that expects you to be professional and request what you want or need. For instance, when I needed equipment, I approached the director and explained my program. I gave her all the points and reasons showing why I needed it and how it would benefit the prison. Do not forget to show, as specifically as you can, how it will benefit the person you're asking or the program they run. You may be surprised at how successful you will be.

Eventually people began to ask me for personal training sessions and even offering me payment. But there were others who trained and I had to be careful. I was mindful of the unwritten rules of the prison environment, and I did not want to step on a hustle as I would damage my relationships if I broke the rules. It was fine, as I could not have added anything onto my schedule anyway. In addition to teaching, I had drug rehab from 12:00 - 3:30, Monday through Friday, as well as computer class and Spanish. I had also started playing soccer and running the soccer league. As I mentioned earlier, I had played soccer as a kid and I rediscovered that passion in prison. Plus, we were winning. I wasn't about to put that on hold!

One afternoon the recreation supervisor approached me. He had been having problems with the girl who ran step class, and he wanted to give me a cardio class and move my other class to the 6:00 pm slot. Jessie suggested a circuit class, so we grabbed all of our fitness magazines and designed a class of forty stations with one minute of exercise at each. I loved having the chance to be creative, and she loved designing the whole floor plan.

Not everything went perfectly. Jessie was outspoken and some of the staff didn't like her attitude or mouth. For the first few weeks it was difficult to get her out early for dinner. Then, one of the officers wouldn't let us in to get our equipment until half an hour before our class, making it tough to finish setting up for forty stations. Though this is true on the outside as well of course, it is even more important in prison to remember that whatever new responsibilities you plan to take on, think beforehand about the challenges and personalities you will have to deal with, and figure out how you will respond. To put it nicely, it is a great way to practice your people skills! When it gets tough, which it will, you will have practiced responses to draw on. Carefully, I'll add.

Despite the challenges, my new class was a hit. People were ready for something new and we were proud that our class was something you would see in a real gym. It worked the whole body, and between our class two days per week, the weekend class, and the step class, there were six days per week of variety exercise including toning and cardio, with a yoga class on weekends.

If you couldn't get fit here, you weren't serious. I had set up a real gym routine and system in prison, with free instructors providing inmates with tips for diet and help in the weight room. I finally had something to be proud of.

Ok, now it's your turn. Look around. Look back at the exercises you did for this chapter. Where can you start? How can you use this place to get where you want to be on the way out, to give yourself something to be proud of, to accomplish while you are here and use once you leave?

Stop reading and write it down. Try to avoid general statements such as "I'll work out more!" That's a start, but be specific. What will you do this week? Which days, which hour in the day? Who can you talk to about creating a plan? As you create your plan for fitness and diet, what else does your facility offer that can push you toward a pursuit or professional interest you can continue to pursue on the outside? Look back at my tips for creating a daily and weekly inventory to track accomplishments and goals. This will be especially important when setbacks occur. If you can get down just one accomplishment on a bad day, hold onto that to keep yourself moving forward on the next day.

CHAPTER 6

HALFWAY HOUSE TO HOME CONFINEMENT: MAKING THE TRANSITION

While it is tough to get healthy in a prison environment, it is actually easier to get healthy while you're locked up than it is to maintain it once you leave. According to a Report from the Re-entry Policy Council, two million Americans are serving time in prison. Ninety-seven percent of those people will be released at some point, and about two out of every three people released from prison in the U.S. are rearrested within three years of their release.iii I know, it's crazy right?!

Why did I think I would be any different? Why would you? I'm not sure why I was, maybe in part because I knew the statistics and was determined not to become that one. By then I had figured out that my life is important. So is yours. I knew it was time to change and because you are reading this, so do you.

Unfortunately, many treatment programs in prison systems across the country are not effective. For example, substance abuse treatment reduces new conviction recidivism by 2.4%. Less than 50% of substance abuse interventions reduce both new conviction and total recidivism.iv Programs had little effect on prison population, operational cost savings, and overall crime reduction. To me, the conclusion to draw from this is not that we should abandon treatment programs. The people who run them, and we, the inmates, do have to genuinely, bravely and consistently address problems of addiction and past patterns before returning to our home environments, which are full of emotional triggers and easily available drugs. To me, the conclusion to draw here is that even if you make great strides while incarcerated (Yay you! Keep going!), the inner work you do in prison just isn't enough to keep you from going straight back to prison soon after you're out. The transition will be tough, and you have to expect that. You have to plan ahead to anticipate the challenges and be even more vigilant than ever in the first few years after you get out. I hope that in reading about my own struggle with the transition, you may find ways to avoid some of the pitfalls and continue healing.

I graduated from the drug program in Connecticut and was released in March, 2010 to a halfway house on Massachusetts Avenue in Boston. From what I could tell, at least half of the women there were using. As is the case in many halfway houses, I was surrounded by drugs and crime.

But I did not go back to drugs. As I said earlier, I still had not solved every emotional problem that had led to my drug abuse and I still wrestle with some of those issues today. I had made a resolute decision to stay clean, but a lot of people do that and still go back. It must have been my firm commitment to fitness and health that kept me out. It was a decision I renewed every day when I worked out and taught other women.

Just before I transitioned out, my biggest concern was whether I would have access to a gym. For the first three days after I arrived, I was required to stay in the house, so I ran in place and did toning exercises. I wasn't going to get much stronger during this time, but that was fine. My goal for these days was just to stay focused, to avoid losing the ground I had gained. This is perfectly ok if it's all you can do in the first few days.

On the third day I was allowed to go to the store and to check out a gym. I chose the Boston Sports Club about a half-mile away. After being locked up for three years, it was like heaven! With more than enough machines, there were weights, classes, a pool and everything I could want. The $125 monthly cost was expensive for me, but I knew it was my lifeline. If you can't afford a gym, see if there are any YMCAs or a Boys' Club that will be willing to help or use lockdown workouts provided. You can always run outside if you need to. If you are determined, you can make it work.

I signed up, informed my counselor and went over the house rules for attending the gym. I was given one hour to attend the gym every day, with thirty minutes for travel time each way. This actually gave me an hour and a half at the gym if I jogged there and back. At the time I was working at my boyfriend Sam's office (I'll write more about him later), and I left for the gym every day at 6:00 am. I was back at the halfway house by 8:00 am, where I stretched, showered and left for work around 8:30 am. My commute was almost an hour, and I arrived to start my workday at 10:00 am. I attended the gym six days per week. I did weights and cardio, changing up my routine often to make my body work hard. I felt terrific.

Eating right at the halfway house was tough. We were not allowed to have food in any room but the kitchen, and we were only allowed in the kitchen at meal times, three times per day. I was used to five or six meals per day. Most staff would let me store unopened food such as protein or granola bars in the kitchen. I would sneak one upstairs, sometimes with an apple for between-meal snacks.

Our food came from a homeless shelter, and there was only one choice of fruit (apples). There were never fresh vegetables, and the ones provided were from a can and overcooked. We had chicken most of the time for meat, which was fine. Despite the bland diet, I did my best to stay fit and make the right choices.

I had the same breakfast every day: oatmeal and fruit. For lunch I bought a protein bar and had a piece of fruit with a sandwich. I had fruit or some other kind of healthy snack between lunch and dinner, and at dinner I would usually have whatever meat they provided along with the vegetable.

By April, 2010 I had spent one month and a week at the halfway house, and I began studying to be a personal trainer. At the gym I was still doing a variety of workouts. Some days I would do an hour on the elliptical or treadmill, then do a core workout including sit-ups, leg raises and planks. On other days I would do thirty minutes of cardio and an hour of either lower or upper body strength training, alternating weight training days.

Depending on your situation, you may or may not have the same amount of time I did. As I mentioned, I went to the gym before I went to work. If you want to succeed, you have to fit it in somewhere. If you tell me your schedule does not leave you enough time, I'll say that if you have time to watch TV, you have time to work out. Maybe you need a workout buddy to help with the motivation, which is fine. Just make sure they are as motivated as you are, if not more. The best thing you can do for yourself is to use the time that you used to fill with using and partying as time to learn, eat right and exercise.

I followed all the rules, although at times I was still treated by some halfway house employees in ways that made me bristle. I had never been good with confrontational approaches even when they were well intended, and I had to make a conscious decision to use what rankled me to try even harder.

Because women exit prison into a variety of locations and environments, the approach that worked for me won't be exactly the same for you. What is important to know is that you can do this. It is possible in whatever transitional environment you face immediately after getting out.

If you are unable to attend a gym, you may use the workouts in Part II of this book. They work in any situation because they are all bodyweight exercises. If you are able to run, go for it! There is nothing like a good run to clear your head and make you feel better. It's great cardio exercise and most people who run will agree it is the perfect time to work through whatever problems you are dealing with in life. If you aren't yet ready to run, try speed walking to start. Both activities give you needed time to be honest with yourself and let the answers and ideas you're looking for come to mind.

CHAPTER 7

DEALING WITH SETBACKS (EVEN BIG ONES)

Setbacks will happen to the best of us. For me, it happened when two officers showed up at my home when I was living with Sam.

"Urine test," one said. They both walked around my living room, touching things and asking questions about the people in our pictures. Sam had just brewed me some coffee, and, in front of the officers, he added some vanilla extract to flavor it as he always did. After urinating in front of the female officer, I gave them the urine sample and was happy to see them go.

One week later, I heard the office door slam and two officers rushed in, right in front of my boss (Sam's business partner). They took me outside, cuffed me and swooped me off to the Barnstable County Jail.

I sat in a chair in the cliché of the dimly lit room, staring up at the officer who wore something that looked like a federal Special Forces uniform. I felt like an accused terrorist.

"You failed your urine test," the officer said, his voice matter-of-fact.

"That's impossible. Noooo!" I said, feeling the tears come. I had come so far and did not understand what was happening.

He dropped the matter-of-fact tone and shifted to sarcasm. "Maybe you had a glass of wine you, uh, forgot about? Needed a drink after a stressful day?" (While on home confinement alcohol is not allowed.)

It wasn't true. I had only been going to work and the gym, studying, eating and sleeping. But why should he listen to me? To him I was only an addict, and addicts lie. My protests about the injustice and impossibility of it all fell on disbelieving ears.

I was sent to Barnstable County Jail. I was not told what would happen. I was allowed to use the phone though. I called everyone I could. I spoke to my mother and retraced my steps of the week before, mentioning when she asked what I had eaten that I had put vanilla extract into my coffee just before the test. She called her friend, a nurse who said vanilla extract had likely been the culprit. Maybe you would have known that, and maybe I should have, but I didn't.

By the time I got to speak to a discipline officer, I was relieved and eager to clear up the mistake. It did not go well. Though he had not met me before, he insisted that an alcoholic would know that vanilla has alcohol in it. I was devastated. All the work I'd done…it hurt badly. And, I was angry. I argued. Who in their right mind would knowingly drink alcohol when she knew she was about to take a urine test? I also wondered about the fact that the two officers had been standing right in front of me when I poured the vanilla in my coffee. Why hadn't they warned me? Hadn't they noticed? Had they seen and not known this would skew the test? Or—the possibility that made me most angry–had they seen, known it would taint the test and chosen to say nothing?

The discipline officer said he was used to dealing with a certain type of person, that I was that type and that he had to find me guilty.

I was kept in segregation for about six weeks. This was a county jail and I was a federal inmate so they did not want anything to happen to me while in their custody. I can't remember a time when I'd ever been more depressed. I was lonely, the food was full of carbs and other empty calories and there were cakes or cookies with every meal. The first two days I ate everything on the tray, feeling sorry for myself and sinking deeper into depression and anger about the unfairness of it all. I was locked inside for twenty-three hours a day and they did not give me a full hour at a time solely for recreation. We had to use the hour we had to exercise, use the phone and shower.

Fortunately, my mini-downward spiral got old quickly as my body felt terrible with what I was doing to it. I coached myself, urging myself to maintain my physical health. I needed it if I wanted to keep my mental health. It took everything I had (including some of my simmering anger) but I designed a workout routine and every day I dragged myself out of that bed to follow it. I washed myself and my clothes in my cell's sink so personal hygiene time did not consume my workout hour. I was not going to let the system break me!

Eventually, I was let into the general prison population and put in a room with a crack addict who kept me up at night being loud and inconsiderate. One day a fellow inmate told me she had said she intended to "use me for my commissary," or hustle me into giving her the funds I had for commissary. Basically, she would be nice to my face and tell sob stories about her life trying to manipulate me into giving her stuff; she would go behind my back and talk about me. Eventually, she began to taunt me openly and regularly.

I had been boiling mad to begin with, and until now I had been using that anger to fuel my workouts. I decided she had made a mistake to single me out for abuse, and one day when we were locked in the room for clean-up, she began taunting me. That day I had been mentally and emotionally ready to snap. After my first time in prison, I had reasoned that as long as I did everything I was supposed to do, as long as I focused on staying healthy and becoming financially independent, I would never be back in prison. But despite everything I had done right, here I was. I felt robbed, angry with the system and angry with her. It all came to the surface as she ranted on about nonsense, and I was ready to leap from my top bunk and attack her. She must have seen the wild look in my eyes, because right before I lost it she suddenly mentioned she had Hepatitis C, which stopped me dead in my tracks. The next day I was moved into a room with a nice, quiet girl, but for an unrelated reason. My cell mate was in the drug program at that facility and had been ordered to share a cell with another inmate in the same program. I thanked fate, as who knows what would have happened if I had attacked her.

About two weeks later, I was moved to the Wyatt Federal Detention Facility in Rhode Island. Barnstable was the county contracted for home confinement, and since I was no longer on home confinement, the feds still had custody of me. I knew a few girls there from prison and was slowly coming out of my funk. The facility and food were much better as well. There was a small recreation area attached, where I would run for thirty to sixty minutes per day. There were also some hydraulic machines for strength training, which made my days a little better.

As had happened in other facilities, my active drive inspired people to get in better shape, and before I knew it I was teaching others again. I continued to struggle with my anger at being sent to prison when I had not knowingly done anything wrong. I finally learned to let that go, chalking it up to "everything happens for a reason." But it was still a setback. I can say now that whatever your setbacks have been and are in the future, do something every day that moves you—even if only a little—in the direction in which you want to go. Eventually, something will come out of it that you need, even if it isn't what you expected.

One day I was working out at the gym, showing a girl how to use the leg extension machine while lifting weights in my own workout, and we started sharing stories. After we worked out together and sat down for a meal she said, "You know what Ferns? You should write a book!"

Every day in Wyatt Detention Facility we had a three-hour lockdown. That day, on a few napkins I had available in my cell, I wrote the first words.

CHAPTER 8

RELATIONSHIPS (UGH...)

Any addict knows that our toughest challenges are in our relationships. This may be true for non-addicts as well, at least among those who have landed themselves in prison. In far too many cases, we do not come from a cushion of healthy relationships that have created healthy personalities who know how to deal with life's challenges.

I was no different than anyone else who had made poor choices in life. Throughout my incarceration I had stayed in contact with an ex-boyfriend Sam (not his real name but the one I said I'd get back to), and we were planning to reunite once I came home. We had dated on and off during my life as an addict, but by the time I was ready to come home I had made huge changes to myself and my life. Could I navigate a new relationship with the same person when I was so changed? Everything about me was different: my goals, dreams, even my daily thoughts.

As I mentioned earlier, when I moved to the halfway house, I got a job in Sam's office. While we seemed to be doing ok, I was still terrified when it was time to come back to society on the home confinement bracelet. I was just getting to know myself and now I was going to be living with someone. He cared about me, but he had always been overprotective, insecure and controlling. When I moved in with him after I transitioned into the halfway house, I felt like a stranger in my own life. I had not been sober that long since I had been fourteen. I had become self-aware through extensive therapy and rehabilitation, and the old me was just that: a person of the past.

Professionally, I had made it out better than when I went in, and my drive could not be contained. Sam did not know how to handle it. He was happy to have the new person I had become, but he continued to try hover over me as he had needed to before I knew how to live my own life well. This bothered me, as after more than three years without privacy, what I longed for most was to be left alone. Feeling smothered, I tried my best to figure it all out and to make him happy.

I also had known before prison that I was bisexual, and I had been involved in a few relationships with women while inside. I had become close to Jessie, a woman I had met in the compound at Danbury. I had been in the drug program at the time, and while I had not been looking for a romantic relationship, being with her had helped stave off loneliness and we had spent a lot of time together. My feelings for her had not fizzled since leaving, and my relationship with her would turn out to be a huge turning point for me in my choice of future partners.

While Sam had no problem with me being with other women and was not threatened by my relationship with Jessie, she did not feel the same way about Sam. I never deceived either of them about the other, but I spent a lot of time confused about my feelings of love for both of them.

She was intelligent and knew all of my weaknesses. The problem was, she often used that knowledge against me, delivering verbal daggers that conflicted with my views of the good in her. Over time (and this was not as easy as it may sound) I came to see her as a teacher for me in that she taught me how to identify patterns that were not good for me, and to walk away from people who treated me poorly when they felt angry or insecure. It was only with extensive therapy that I was able to figure this out and let it go so that it would not continue to trigger feelings and responses that made me vulnerable to drug use again.

While the advice I'll give next may not be anything new, I cannot urge you strongly enough to look at the damaging people and situations you have invited and allowed to be in your life. What do they have to teach you? If it is how to walk away from someone who is not good for you, what if the only way to learn that is by actually doing it?

Yes, this is harder than it sounds, and none of it happened in a snap for me either. When Sam saw a nasty letter that Jessie had written about him, he was no longer supportive of that relationship, and he gave me the ultimatum that it was either her or him. I did not handle it well and continued to communicate with her while telling Sam I had ended it.

I know. What a mess. I should have known better, but it was months before I stopped communicating with her behind his back. She continued to make me miserable, and I found myself putting walls up that I had thought I'd left behind in prison. I deceived myself as well, feeling strong as I distanced myself from all my emotions by focusing 100 percent on school, projects, volunteer work and hobbies. I lost my desire to be touched or nurtured, which was something I had always wanted more than anything else. It even felt empowering to lose what I would describe at the time as my biggest weakness: my neediness. Most people entering sobriety seem to see feelings rise to the surface with their newfound sobriety. That wasn't true for me. I lost mine.

Maybe it was what I needed at the time, as it helped me to finish school and do work that I believed was important. But in the end, we do not have to choose between being loved and achieving what we want for our lives. We can actually have both.

Eventually I broke off communication with Jessie. But I still had more to learn in my relationship with Sam, which by then had fallen into a comfortable routine. I loved our friendship, but I never felt like I could be honest with him due to his sensitive and sometimes controlling nature. I felt trapped. There was a time I had seen myself being happy with him, but I had to reconsider when he continued to tell me whom I could and could not talk to.

In the end, the idea that I'd even had a choice to make between Sam and Jessie was something I had constructed myself, maybe to avoid being alone, or to avoid feeling guilty about letting people down by leaving them. Who said I had to choose? It turns out, if neither choice feels right, you have to invent another. I needed to be free from both relationships and consider the hope that there were people with whom I could be myself—independent, free of drugs and able to shape a life that could always be moving forward. I will not say I am free of knee-jerk reactions and attempts to shut myself off from painful emotions, or that I have no problem opening up to people I want to trust. But if I could learn to recognize my own role in my problems, if I could face my deepest emotional obstacles, then you—the women I am writing to right now—can too.

CHAPTER 9

AH, SO THAT'S WHY DETOURS HAPPEN: WRITING A BOOK AND BECOMING A BETTER TRAINER AT WYATT DETENTION FACILITY

My mood immediately improved at Wyatt, where the gym had some hand-me-down equipment from Curves and I had access to the recreation area all day. The food was healthier and the rules were not strict about saving food, so I could still snack between meals. I taught a class four days per week, teaching women two days per week in the equipment room for a forty-five minute circuit, then in the outdoor recreation area for cardio and stretching. The other two days they came out to the recreation area for abs and a cardio boot camp. Women at Wyatt were also instructed to walk for one hour (or run if they could) on the days they didn't have class.

Many women had no exercise experience, so I tried to keep them motivated with positive reinforcement and a gradual easing into the routines. I love to be pushed and to push myself, but here I learned how mindful I have to be as a trainer that not everyone is like that. I had to adapt, to meet women where they were physically and emotionally, or else I would discourage them by pushing too hard. I tried my best to help them change their eating habits, but with so little time there, I did not feel I was able to help as a trainer as much as I had wanted to.

That doesn't mean I thought, even once, "If only I could stay in prison longer!" When I finally was discharged on July 15, 2010, I was glad to be out of there. But I often wondered about the women who were still there, ready to get started or desperately trying to maintain the hard-fought gains they had accomplished and did not want to slip from their fingers. I wanted to continue coaching them. I wanted to reach the women I would never meet. I wanted to reach you. So I kept writing.

Once I was finally discharged, I got a job at Total Fitness gym in Bristol Rhode Island. As may be the case for you, it would not become clear until it was all over and I was making sense of my life backwards: all of my moving around, even the setback which sent me right back to federal prison, had given me knowledge about the various challenges and limitations women face while working to recover their lives in different prison environments. I had to learn the ways fitness and health could be achieved even in places that present the greatest challenges to diet, exercise and mental health. And I had to do it myself. Otherwise, I would not have the knowledge or experience to train you now. Which challenges that you face right now, if you were to overcome them, might yield valuable skills you can use to be successful once you're out?

PART II
YOUR TURN

CHAPTER 10

TIME FOR A PEP TALK

Ok, enough about me (for the most part). Now I am a physical trainer on the outside, and if I do say so myself, I'm a pretty good one! I learned how to be good by working first with myself, then with other incarcerated women and now with a whole bunch of people at various levels of health and fitness at the gym where I work. The rest of this book is about you. While in earlier chapters I gave you a few exercises and diet suggestions that got me started, from this point on you should consider me your long-distance personal trainer as you take your achievements in health and fitness to the next level.

For those of you who have been enjoying the book but have not yet begun a fitness or diet routine, as I said earlier, I know how hard it is to get started while you're locked up. You may feel depressed, lazy and tired. You might say "I'll lose the weight when I get home…" Blah blah blah. Keep telling yourself that if you want to stay miserable.

Now, this isn't the time for shame for any previous excuses you have made for not working out or eating well. Believe me, I've made them too. But do take a look at yourself, stop feeling sorry for yourself and make a commitment to stop making excuses now. Here you are in a facility where you do not want to be. But this place gives you ample time to do this, today, right now. What else do you have to do? Do you brush your teeth every day? Well, that's what exercise needs to become: a regular part of your life. Many of you have been addicts on the street. So was I. They say we trade one addiction for another. If that is the case, why not trade drugs and alcohol for exercise and a healthy diet? I'm not saying you should exercise three to four hours a day or that you can never eat ice cream or pizza again. I'm saying you can grow to love your body, treat it right, get it in shape and get to know how being healthy can filter into and change all aspects of your life. If you had known me before my incarceration, you would never have expected to hear such statements from me. But now that I live it, I love it. And I want to help you get there.

If you honestly want to change and feel good about yourself, I will help you. But ultimately, it is up to you to stick with it. No matter how depressed you may be, exercise will get your endorphins to kick in and boost your mood, relieve stress, and just make your days better. Is an hour of your day so much time? Look where you are and look what you're doing. You're doing time, and now is when you can take the time to better yourself. Do you love yourself?

If you said no, that's okay. That's why I want to work with you through this book, because I absolutely know you can get there.

One thing you will need to do is tell yourself that you will do this. What I mean is that on those days you don't want to (and there may be many at first), you need to tell yourself, "Look, I don't care, I am going to do this!" You may laugh at the idea of talking to yourself, but I have done it many times (especially in segregation)! Who cares? It works. Even if you have to talk yourself out of some bad decisions more than once, it's worth it.

Well yes, you say, of course it would be, if I knew how. But if I've never been motivated to do this before. How do I start now? If I have tried before and failed to become fit, how can I make sure it is real this time?

Good questions. Here's what I suggest. Take out a pen and paper. It's time to ask yourself, what motivates you? Start writing. Here are some of the best motivators I've seen in training people:

1) Your Kids. Do you have children at home missing you? Do you have a child who is sad, doing poorly in school or causing trouble while you're gone? Maybe they're asking themselves why you left them. Even if they are not, what I'm going to say next might upset some of you. That's the point! Are you giving your kids future problems because you haven't straightened out your own life yet? If you don't get your own life right and be the mom you want to be, won't you increase the risk of your kids having mental, emotional and social problems, abandonment issues, addictions or anger problems? As you probably know, the example of your life is more powerful than anything you can ever teach your kids through what you say. Are they going to follow in your footsteps? Who's taking care of them? No one can do that like a mommy or daddy who has their shit straightened out enough to be a good parent, and that means a lot more than mere words telling kids what is right and wrong. Now, what if the example you have set so far isn't so great? And what if that can actually be changed for the better? What if the example you give can instead illustrate how much is possible when someone turns her life around? If any of this applies to you, use it as your motivator. The second you start debating whether you should skip exercising today or eat things that are bad for you, picture your kids. Think of how happy they'll be if you are living the life of which you are capable, and better yet if you come home to them healthy, energetic as a new, positive person. You can use them as your motivation, because they need you at your best.

2) Vanity. Ok, I know some may say if we're not supposed to be vain in the first place this is not the right reason to exercise or eat right. But let's be realistic. Nobody wants to look like shit. I don't care what your 200-pound bunkie tells you. She is not happy being fat! Ladies, stick thin is not in and neither is obese. Healthy is. Everyone looks good when they're healthy.

If vanity and looking good for others is what motivates you, so be it—for now. The rest will fall into place later, when you see how much better healthy feels on the inside and you start caring less what other people think.

3) Your addictive personality. Wait, isn't this bad? After all, it may be the part of you that got you into trouble in the first place and I know not everyone will agree with me on this. But as I said earlier, trading one addiction for another (one with actual health benefits) is better than following the one that took your life into the toilet. Maybe it's not popular to say, but I don't care. I decided to stop smoking cigarettes, sniffing coke, binge drinking, dropping acid, eating mushrooms and blowing all my money at strip clubs. I traded all that for eating healthy, exercising and finding new, creative hobbies. Yes, I can sometimes go overboard even with healthy habits, but I'll take being a mostly happy, always-moving energizer bunny over being miserable in the life I had before. Overall, I spend no more than one to two hours at the gym, five to six days per week. On occasion I eat some unhealthy foods. I just structured my life, and being healthy is like brushing my teeth now. If that's trading addictions, then call it what you will. The funny thing is that all the people who have thrown this at me as a criticism are unhealthy themselves. A drug counselor who lives on caffeine and nicotine, an overweight woman who never has anything nice to say to anyone, an inmate who says the minute she goes out she's going to shoot up coke to slim down! Need I say more? The trade could save your life.

4) Sickness and Death. Yes, I know this sounds morbid as a motivator. But the reality is that there are countless health issues that come along with long-term drug and alcohol use. This alone should motivate you, but that's usually not how it works. Most people don't feel motivated by this until they actually get sick and realize they have something to live for. Even if you don't care if you live or die, feeling like shit is no bargain. Maybe you can be one of the people who doesn't have to face your own death to be motivated by this one, but if not, try starting simply because you're sick of feeling bad. Who wants to get liver damage, cancer, hepatitis, HIV, emphysema (and the list goes on)? When I first drafted this chapter, I could honestly say my brain felt shot, and I can still feel the effects of my drugs as I edit this after being healthy for a few years. But since my lifestyle changed and I starting taking care of my health, I began to feel more clear-headed. Please, start now before things get any worse or you cause irreversible damage. You don't want to add even more regret to life, do you?

5) Your goals. The biggest reason logically is your future, your goals, or who you can picture yourself being in your biggest dreams. This motivation covers everything. You are not invincible. You don't have nine lives, although it may seem that way. You are where you are for a reason. Don't you think that might be a clue that it's time to change? While you're working out, picture what you want your future to be. Keep your most compelling reason for getting well in front of you, imagining your got-it-together self as often as you can and especially when

facing decisions between a healthy and an unhealthy choice. Before you go to eat something crappy, before you skip your workout, think about what is motivating you. Think about your goal. Tell yourself to keep going. Remind yourself that you can. Tell yourself that nothing can stop you. You will get in shape—not tomorrow but today—you will get healthy, and you will change. This is who you are now. This is a part of you. If you can accomplish this, you can do anything. As I said earlier, I don't care how corny it sounds to be talking to yourself (Plus, you don't have to do it out loud!). If the result is looking and feeling great, who cares? You deserve that, but it's not up to anyone else to give it to you. Only you can give that to yourself. No more excuses!

6) Music. Who doesn't like music? The best way to pump yourself up is an upbeat song you can feel. You may not have an iPod in here, but use that walkman. (Yes, they still have walkmans in prison to my knowledge.) It was my best friend. A good song gets me going like nothing else, and when I am feeling the music, I can blow through a workout. Figure out what music gets you going. Hip-hop and techno usually work best for me, but punk music and some alternative rock will do it too. When I am done with a workout that was full of music, I am dripping with sweat. So get something to listen to your favorite upbeat music on, borrowing from someone if necessary (a headset also keeps people from bothering you). If you are near constant talkers and they don't get the picture that you are zoning out in your cardio, you may have to pull your earphones off once or twice—try to be polite no matter how annoying they are—and let them know. "I need all the energy I can get for this workout," you can say, "but I can talk when I'm done!" Don't let anyone take you out of your zone! This is about you and your health. If music works for you, use it anytime your motivation lags and you need a boost to get started. Once you get started, you'll probably keep going.

Now that you have identified your primary motivators, you can use whatever feels right at the time. If one is not working, try another. Throw everything you have at it, because it's time to get to work. First, sit down with pad and paper and identify a time in your day when you can add a workout. Add some kind of physical exercise, walking, whatever is your starting point—into your routine every day. For me, in the morning after breakfast was best. It gets it out of the way and makes you feel fresh and energized. It also seems to make the day go by quickly, and on some days when you're locked up, that is the only thing you want. Others like to work out at the end of the day because it gives them something to look forward to, and when stressful situations come up during the day, they can imagine yourself burning off all the stress later (instead of punching the "stressor" in the face!). Either way, set a time, six days per week at 7:30 am, for example, if breakfast is at 6:00 am. You should have one rest day per week. If you are really trying to lose weight, I suggest you do something easier but still physical, such as walking, on the seventh day.

No matter how hard it is, commit yourself to not letting your circumstance control you. Try to push yourself to do this every day, no matter what, and in almost no time it will become a habit you look forward to. When you pick a time, make it work. Don't pick a time that commissary comes, church goes on, the barber or hair dresser comes, etc. As I drafted this chapter from my cell, a few girls missed class because they had wanted to do their hair. I told them that their body comes first. Their hair could wait. Hair takes an hour, tops. Your body takes months. You need to stay on a strict schedule while you're locked up. If you make excuses and let other distractions get in the way, you will not reach your goal. If you are reading this, chances are that in your mind and heart, you want to do this. So do it. Why not better yourself? This is your time with your body. Don't let anyone or anything take away your commitment to exercise.

Next, you need to think about your diet. What the heck are you eating? Soups, beef sticks, candy, cookies? Stop! There is a whole chapter later on how to plan your diet, but for now, I want to explain food times and give you an idea of how your new habits will help you to succeed.

First off, food is not your enemy. I know how many of us feel that it is, but food is your fuel. That may be sound corny, but stop and think about it for a moment. How often do you put food in your mouth and see either the food or yourself as simply bad, going straight to your stomach where it will turn you into an even bigger blob than you feel you are already? When you eat, with your choices tell yourself that food is your fuel—actually picture it—that your body needs it to function and even to stay lean. How will that thought alone affect what you eat? Pay attention to how a cupcake makes you feel vs. lean protein, yogurt or oats. Pay attention to how long your energy lasts with different food choices. Which foods feel more like fuel? You just need to understand how to feed yourself. Oh, and about all those other methods of slimming down that seem like a faster fix—taking laxatives, wrapping yourself in plastic bags to sweat, eliminating carbs—forget them all. No, it is not easy to eat right when you are incarcerated. I get it, but eating well and exercising are the only way you will get the results you want. You have a choice, and you absolutely can make it work.

Once you plan your fitness time, schedule your eating times. Personally, I found scheduling around institution meal times was the best way to go. For example, if they serve breakfast at 6:30 am, you can work out from 7:30 - 9:00 am, have a small meal around 9:30 am, have lunch between 11:30 am and noon, have a small meal at around 2:30 pm, and eat when they serve dinner at 5:00 pm. If you are hungry after dinner, have a small snack around 8:00 pm, but no later.

Outside the prison walls, you may not want your days to blow by. But in the world behind these walls when we cannot wait to get out, that's exactly what we want. Once I lost the weight and was into my fitness routine, my weeks went by like days. It won't happen immediately, but it does not take as long as you may think to change a habit. When I went to prison, in three months I gained thirty pounds and it took another three months to get back into shape and start looking good. And for all of you people with attitudes of Billy Badass who think you're somebody special—stop fronting and turn the insecurity into drive. Walk the walk. If you can relate to what I'm saying then start now.

As I said above, food is not your enemy. You need to eat, all day. Especially when you're exercising, don't try to skip the fuel your body needs. You just need to eat the right things. You also need to drink a lot of water. According to the Mayo Clinic, women should drink two and half liters per day (about the same in quarts) and men three. When you exercise you will need to replace one and half - two liters depending on the intensity.v No more Kool-Aid, no more soda. Once you get the crap out of your system for a week or so, you will not miss it. In fact, you'll feel your body rejecting unhealthy sugars that just weeks before, you thought you needed.

I can't say how often I hear, "But I hate water!" My response to that was always the same. "Too bad. I hate prison—but unfortunately I'm here."

The next chapters are how we're going to get all of this started for you. Now that your head and strategy are getting on track, let's get your body there.

CHAPTER 11

CREATING AN EXERCISE ROUTINE THAT WORKS IN PRISON

In prison more than anywhere else, to build and maintain fitness you need to use what you have and be creative. What type of facility are you in? If you have access to machines, weights, classes, etc., take advantage of them all week. If you're limited to a small recreation area or stuck in segregation, your plan will be different but no less effective.

To get the results you want, you need to incorporate cardio, muscle toning and stretching. Then make designated days for certain exercises.

Create a fitness journal.

In your journal you will plan your workouts, track your progress and reflect on your fitness and progress. Use template in this chapter to create your own workouts based on your facility's resources and your fitness level. But this is just to get you started so also see the detailed workouts in Chapter fifteen. Throughout the remainder of this book you will see tables and charts to guide you in your workouts and diet. If there are any exercises or terms you haven't heard before, please see the glossary at the end as well as the photos demonstrating the exercises. For your own fitness level, don't be too easy on yourself! You want to be sweating and you want your heart rate to increase. If you want to be exact, check your heart rate while exercising against the American Heart Association's guidelines for target heart rate for your age. If you're trying to lose weight, you also need to be building your muscles. For women who are worried that they will "get bulky," remember that muscle helps burn fat. Don't listen to all that jazz about getting too big.

Why all the charts? One thing you will notice about this book is that I use a lot of charts to get people started on workout routines and diets. I do it and advise you to do it, because it works. If you keep the written exercise routine with you while you work out, it helps you to finish the whole thing. If you try to just put a workout in your head and wing it, you're more likely to quit before you're done, skip undesirable exercises and cut down time. Always finish everything. Even if you need to take it slow, finish, finish, finish. By doing the whole thing, you train yourself to be motivated. I started writing down things to force myself to finish on those days

I just didn't feel like it. When it was over, I was always glad I pushed through. The charts and routines can guide you, motivate you and help you begin and maintain your healthy lifestyle.

In the next chapter on diet, you will notice that I also use food charts, so I'll say this now too: yes, you need to do it! Jot down everything related to exercise and diet to track your progress. You can give yourself credit for every push-up in your journal, but you also can't skip writing down the cake you ate in that journal. Only you are seeing this, and you need to see where you need improvement. Make this a priority and sit with it after every meal. Plan your meals and in-between meals ahead of time. I'll say more on that later.

As you'll see, exercise is only half of the commitment. You will have to eat better and there is no compromising in that. So use the charts for food and exercise, especially because you don't have a personal trainer physically available. While I am your trainer through this book now, I'm trying to show you a way to be your own trainer.

This plan is just to get you started and give you an idea of what's worked for me. Your strength and level will determine the weight you should use and the intensity of your cardio endurance. You may modify any of the weights and cardio levels to suit your needs. If you've never exercised much and are overweight, start by using weights and a less intense cardio routine. In order to build up your cardio endurance, begin slowly. Let's say your track is large and four times around is ½ mile. Try walking ¾ of a lap and jog the last quarter. When you've completed one mile, you'll have jogged a quarter mile. Every week add a quarter mile more. If you can do more, do it. Always set a small goal and try to surpass it. An example would be to say, "Today I will repeat a two—lap cycle–one walking, one jogging—for an hour." When you're transitioning from the jogging lap into a walking one, try to jog into half of the next walking lap.

If you're on a machine and you want to get off, or if you are tired or bored, tell yourself that you only have so many minutes or miles left (whichever feels more manageable). As I've said, this is a starter plan for people with access to equipment. You may add whatever exercises you'd like. Just write it down and carry your plan with you.

Workout for County Jail and Prisons Without Weights

The plan below is based on a county that has what I like to call a universal tree, which many counties have in their recreation areas. It includes pull-up bars, a Roman chair, reverse Roman chair and push-up handle. If your facility has a universal tree, this workout is designed for you. If you're not sure what each piece of equipment is, ask.

I am not suggesting you use anything that is contraband, but if you have a room and can put some books in a towel without getting into any trouble, or if you can improvise with medicine balls, you should use the additions in some of your exercises. See the photos in this book for examples. I know most counties don't have machines or large running tracks. This is where you need to have will and drive to get through your cardio. As you know now, I did cardio in segregation, so I know if you want it badly enough you can do this. Being able to stick with this throughout your incarceration is going to keep you focused and strong upon release. Please believe me. You can do this. Try this weekly plan to start:

I know most counties don't have machines or large running tracks. This is where you need to have will and drive to get through your cardio. As you know now, I did cardio in segregation, so I know if you want it badly enough you can do this. Being able to stick with this throughout your incarceration is going to keep you focused and strong upon release. Please believe me. You can do this. Try this weekly plan to start:

Cardio

The cardio portion of your workouts is suggested for you in charts throughout this book, and because everyone is at different levels, I will provide multiple plans in Chapter Fifteen. These are basic examples of facility plans for you to utilize at your level.

Getting cardio right in counties is a challenge. Here's what I've found works for me: if there is a recreation area that provides machines, use them. If your facility has workout videos, use them. Having someone to walk through things is a great motivator. Also, keep this in mind: don't worry about "looking stupid." Many people will have things to say about people trying to better themselves. They may be insecure or jealous, or they may just have problems of their own that have nothing to do with you. What I used to say was, "I may look like a fool bouncing around, but I look damn good naked!" That shuts people up. Or when people came to my class and spectators had something negative to say, I'd say, "Why are you on the sidelines talking smack instead of playing the game?" That usually worked for me, and sometimes it even got someone to join us.

If there are no machines or videos, do what you can with what you have. At times I had a recreation yard, but it was small so I jogged laps. Boring? Yes. But I wanted to look and feel good, and I just kept telling myself this would get me a few steps closer to that goal. To stay motivated, you may be allowed to listen to music. If not, count your laps or let your mind wander. Depending on your fitness level, it may take about forty-five minutes to jog 200-225 laps. I started by setting a goal of one-hundred laps. No matter how I felt, I did it, talking to myself when I needed to: "Only twenty to go."

Lower Body	Upper Body	Abs / Back
- 2 sets of 20 1 leg dead lifts - 2 sets of 25 squats - 2 sets of 25 calf raises - 2 sets of 25 inner thigh leg lifts - 3 sets of 10 lunges, back foot elevated on a bench - Repeat - Cardio 30-60 minutes - Stretch	- 3 sets of 10 push-ups - 3 sets of 10 tricep dips - 3 sets o pull-ups, until failure - 3 sets of 10 push offs - Repeat - Cardio 30-60 minutes - Stretch	- 50 crunches - 2 sets of 20 oblique crunch - 3 sets of 10 Roman chair leg lifts - 3 sets of 10 reverse Roman chair - 3 sets of 10 supermen - Repeat - Cardio 30-60 minutes - Stretch

Also, you do not have to jog for the whole time. First, figure out your level. Don't just jump into three-hundred laps from nothing. It takes time. For instance, if you're just starting out, for twenty to thirty minutes, alternate between walking five laps and jogging one, or try fifty laps. As I've said, counting laps works great for me. It's how I push through. A good way to push yourself is to set a goal, let's say twenty laps, then push past it to do twenty-five. You will feel so much better. Each time you go out there, push harder—even when you don't feel like it. Once you are about halfway through it will be so much easier.

Finally, your tolerance and fitness levels will build more quickly than you think. The first month will be the most difficult, but for your own sake you must get through it. Even if you need to walk for a while, then run, just keep moving enough to break a sweat and feel your heart rate increase to something that's uncomfortable but not painful.

Repeat Day 1	Repeat Day 2	Abs / Back	Day Off
		- 50 sit ups 3 sets of 10 leg lifts - 50 side bends each side - 3 sets of 10 supermen - 3 sets of 10 reverse Roman chair Repeat	- Walk

Recreation Yard Cardio Routine, Advanced:

On Page fifty-nine is an example of a recreation yard cardio routine to keep things interesting. As I've said, having a chart to go by is a good way to motivate yourself and get through these routines. For me it's the only way I kept up my routines in counties. In prisons it is easier. If you can't stay with it in prison, then you really don't want it. But even though it is harder in county/segregation, when you do it you will feel amazing. Try this:

See the glossary and photos in the appendix if you're not sure what the exercise names mean. See the chapter on workouts for more detailed workouts that progress from one level to the next.

Stretching

Whether you are losing weight, body building or just staying fit, you need to stretch! It is just as important as the exercise itself because it prevents injury so you can keep working out, and it makes you feel so much better which will also keep you motivated. The best time to stretch is after your workout. When I wake up in the morning I like to do what I call the nature stretch. It's just that. I do what feels natural. It's nothing crazy, just something to loosen up my body a little bit. I just stretch my arms up, bend down, touch my toes, twist a little, and roll my neck. After my workout and while my muscles are still warm, I set aside five to ten minutes to stretch. I combine simple, intuitive stretches with a few yoga poses.

> ### Laps & Exercises
> Walk 2 laps, jog 10 laps, walk 2 laps
> Do 50 jumping jacks, 20 mountain climbers
> Walk 1 lap, jog 10 laps
> Do 20 spidermen, 50 count footballs
> Walk 1 lap, jog 10 laps
> Do 10 burpees, 50 jumping jacks

So many people don't stretch and end up with avoidable injuries that make it harder to move forward with their goals. Plenty of people get hurt and then feel frustrated and depressed because they are out of commission. Then they turn to food again. You can avoid this mistake, and a good start would be to review the photos and stretch chart in the back of the book.

One more thing for those who think stretching is a waste of time: while stretching can be a relaxing reward to a workout, any kind of movement always burns more calories than sitting still. So please don't skip your stretching!

Finally, I would like to stress that you do not want to do the same routine every day. Even when you do weights, change it up daily to work different muscle groups, but have it all in the plan. I will include copies of my own personal plans later. Just know that wherever you are, you need a routine in front of you.

Using Your Facility

All facilities are different, and the important thing to remember is to ask questions and take advantage of whatever your facility has to offer.

Most prisons offer a nutrition class. Take it, and make it a priority to incorporate the advice into your routine as much as possible. There are usually exercise classes, boot camps, weight training, etc. Put together a routine utilizing these classes.

> **Laps & Exercises**
>
> Walk 1 lap, jog 10 laps
>
> Do 20 mountain climbers, 50 count footballs, 50 jumping jacks,
>
> 20 spidermen, 10 burpees
>
> Walk 2 laps, jog 10 laps, walk 2 laps and stretch

If there is boot camp on the weekends, take it. On the weekdays you can follow one of the plans I gave above or do a cardio day one day, weights/cardio the next, repeat and then take a day off. Let's say there's a circuit class four nights a week. Take it. On the weekends they offer body training. Take that too, and then take one day off. For people who really need a class setting, most prisons offer enough classes to organize a schedule that will fill up six days a week. What the heck, it's free for you! In the free world people spend a month's rent at a time to get fit. In most prisons you can get the same classes or close to them for free. Also, there are people who can help you. Equipment, videos, use them all.

On top of your workouts, prisons always have sports. But remember, this is prison, not the Olympics. Try something even if you didn't play on the street. Try basketball, volleyball, soccer, racquetball, baseball, whatever. It is all great exercise.

When you're ready to complain, remember that in the prisons you have a much better situation than someone in holding or county has. When you are in holding or county, remind yourself that at least you're not in lock. When you're in lock, read my chapter on lock! You can be fit almost anywhere.

Fitness Etiquette

"I'm incarcerated, so why do I need etiquette?"

During a workout one day, another inmate inspired me to write this section. I had my mat and a ball that I had retrieved from the closet to do the circuit routine I always did on Tuesdays.

As I was done running my laps, I went to the area to use the ball, and another inmate asked, "Can I use this?" Before I had a chance to answer, she tried to get on the ball. I told her I'd be done at 9:15. But the second I was done with my jumping jacks to go back to the ball, she was on it doing sit-ups. I told her there was another ball in the closet.

"Why don't you go and get it?" I asked her. She got up and gave me a dirty look. Instead of putting it back where it belonged when she was finished, this lady let it roll all over the place, annoying everyone as it got into their paths as they walked and ran. She showed no consideration for anyone else, and I knew from being in the gym frequently the only time she ever used the balls were when others had brought them out to use them. Then she proceeded to interrupt others' routines. This was someone who actually made an effort to defy etiquette. But there are also people who have zero etiquette because they are just oblivious. Read this and you won't have to be either of those annoying people.

Something I want to warn you about is jealousy and negativity, which you may notice or experience more often now that you are taking the initiative to better yourself. As you know, there is a lot of negativity in your environment. I know it takes a huge effort to ignore it sometimes, but you must. Steer clear! People who have no drive, don't care about anyone else, or are just plain miserable will always have something negative to say. When these people come around, ignore them, work around them, keep the headphones in and do whatever it takes to stay out of their negative space. Make like you don't see them, as at times they will go out of their way to push your buttons. Eventually, they do go away when they can't get a rise out of you. When you're annoyed and wondering how that long will take, just remind yourself that other people's issues are not worth ruining your health and freedom for. People used to make fun of me, get in my way, move equipment or leave it lying around thoughtlessly, and do as much ignorant shit as they could to get a rise out of me. I learned to outlast and ignore them. If it helps, in the moment ask yourself where people like that are going to be in five years. Where will they get in life? The people who caused those kinds of problems for people when I was in prison are probably miserable still. Overweight, strung out, whatever. Do not let them get in the way of your goals to look and feel better. People will only start improving once they are fed up enough with their own current lives to see the role they are playing in their own misery. Until they get there, those people who are most insecure about themselves are the people who talk smack and cause trouble. We know it and they know it. All they do is talk because that's all they can do from the daily perspective of misery. Remember that when you're feeling at the end of your rope in dealing with someone like that.

Now, if you are that negative person, you can change that. Try boosting your self-esteem and doing something to better yourself (if you're reading this book, that's a start), rather than bad mouthing or sabotaging people who are.

Let me share a few more pointers on etiquette. You do not own the equipment. If there is not enough equipment, such as weights, we all have to share them. We are not children and don't need to fight like them! Be a positive person in your fitness lifestyle. Come on, did you buy these things? I'm not saying stop your workout to lend someone something you're using. I'm saying that if you're not using something that there are only a few of, then share. If I have three different sized weights, and someone is looking for, let's say, a forty-pound bar, and I'm not using the twenty-pound bar at the moment, why do I need to say no, you can't use it because I am? I can grow up and figure out a way to share it. There is no need to hog equipment.

Nor is there a need to use equipment someone else is using when something else is available. I've seen some of the most ignorant things in the weight room in prison. Around 8:00 am one weekday morning, there were about three of us in the weight room in Danbury. We were using three of the four flat benches. We each had a few weights with us in our areas. So everyone was doing her thing, and a girl who was new to the facility walked in. She looked around, and mind you, there were two racks full of free weights since there were only three of us in there. Although she could have used them, instead she walked over to the area we were using and grabbed two ten-pound dumbbells from the weights we were using. The girl went to a vacant area, did a few sets, put them down, and left the weight room. Not only could she have used other weights that were available without interrupting somebody else's workout, but she could have given them back when she was finished. Please, people, this is common sense! If there is plenty of equipment available, don't go over to where someone else is working out and take stuff they might be using. It's basically the Golden Rule for weight rooms. Treat others as you want to be treated. Have some consideration and use your brains.

As I mentioned, some people are negative and will try to get a rise out of you or start trouble. Do your best to practice humility. For example, one day I was in the weight room with three or four others. I put my gloves on the bench near my water and some weights I was using. I went to the bathroom, and when I came back a woman who was known to be a miserable person had thrown my gloves off the bench and had her feet hanging over my water jug using the weights I had gotten for myself off the rack (which was full of other weights I might add). Now I could have made a big deal and told her off. Instead I retrieved my stuff including the weights from the floor she was not using, and moved to a vacant bench. About five minutes later she threw the weights on the floor and left. The funny thing about it was that she kept looking over at me. Clearly her intention was to get a rise out of me, but I was not going to let her win and rob my own peace of mind. So I ignored her the whole time. I know you've been there, when someone is just digging into you trying to get you to take the bait. And honestly, that scenario could have gone in any direction at different times in my life. I've been called a punk by many people for not speaking up about things. I don't personally feel that I'm better; I just don't need to stoop to that level. Frankly, neither should you. Who are these people? Are they worth the headaches they are trying to cause? Hell no. I'm here to better myself and you are here to better yourself. People, you are getting healthy and taking steps toward a better you! Don't let evil or negative people stop you. After all, you don't want to be doing the seg workout if you don't have too, right?

Have fitness etiquette and ignore those who don't. If you must say something, try not to stoop to a negative person's level or allow yourself to get sucked into an unnecessary conflict. For example, "Hey, I'm trying to better myself here, minding my own business. I don't have time to chat, thanks." Put your headset on and ignore them. Most of the time, like a fly, the person will go away. A lot of people have emotional and mental problems in prison and they need attention. Don't play into it. Worry about you. This all ties into your success, I promise you this. So set an example by being able to control your own self and focus on your own health. One thing that helped me to do this was keeping my radio on loud enough so I could ignore all the negativity in the air. All you need to do is worry about you and be civil. I'm pretty friendly by nature so I would "kill them with kindness." That's how my etiquette works. Just focus on what you are doing and be considerate of others and the equipment. I know it is easier said than done sometimes, but this is a big part in your lifestyle change and it all ties together. Your attitude is everything. In fact, in ways you probably can't even imagine yet, just like a negative attitude can contaminate everything, your new positive focus can spill over into all sorts of areas of your life, from fitness and professional goals to personal relationships.

Note to Obsessives (You know who you are): Don't overdo it!

For all of you obsessive people, I am not preaching. I have this problem as well and I always have to be mindful and create a balance for myself. One lady I know walks in the morning, does my class at 1:30 pm, then later I see her in the indoor gym on the resistance machines. I told her to calm it down a little. She never takes a day off. I explained to her that she needs to let her body have at least one rest day. Who knows if she will listen, but I explained to her that if she never gives her body time to heal, she won't get the results she wants.

Another woman I know was in the weight room constantly. She did all kinds of exercises, sets and reps. Variety is good, but she was clearly overdoing it. She asked me why she was not getting results. Why wasn't she getting definition in her muscles? Spending two hours in the weight room every single day was likely a big part of the reason. Everybody is different, but I don't spend crazy amounts of time in the weight room, and I'm toned. I don't ever take more than two days off, but I give my body one full day off a week. I change up my routines and my muscles feel it after a workout, but there is no need to overwork your body. If you cause an injury by overdoing it, that can really set you back, especially if you're prone to depression or tend to get lazy, as it's tougher to get started again after falling out of the routine of exercising.

People who try to rush results always end up slowing themselves down. If you are overweight, there's nothing wrong with taking a thirty to sixty minute walk and doing a routine in the same day. Some of my trainees would be out walking in the morning and doing class for an hour in the afternoon. There is a difference in wanting it badly and overdoing it. Live a healthy lifestyle, but please be aware of and manage your obsessions if you tend to overdo things.

CHAPTER 12

PLANNING A DIET THAT FUELS YOU

One of the things I learned while incarcerated was that there are so many women who have no clue how to eat right. If you are one of them, don't feel bad. If you do know about nutrition and you eat bad food anyway, now is the time to stop rationalizing. For example, cheese that looks neon orange or comes out of a can is not good for you, whether you call it cheese or not. Besides the fact that I went to school for nutrition, my parents made me eat healthy foods growing up, so I've always had some idea of what was good and bad to eat. It is okay if you were never taught or you just didn't care. But that was then. Now, it's time to care. Start with a food journal, writing everything down that you eat.

As I said earlier, I know how hard it is to eat healthy when you're locked up. But let's just get one thing straight: not only do you need to eat all day, but you have to make good choices. Not Ramen noodles, beef sticks, cookies, and chips. Real food. We can all agree that the commissary is not exactly Whole Foods, but we can still work with what we have.

Depending on where you are now with your diet, you can determine how to get started. I know a lot of you want this but get sidetracked easily; when that tray lands in front of you, all bets are off. We need to change that. Many of the women I worked with struggled in this area at first but are now doing a great job. What I suggested for them was to cut some things out of their diets slowly, while others (butter!) could go right away. For example, on some days we were given three pancakes and two sausages. I told them to eat two pancakes and one sausage, leaving off the butter and using just a small amount of syrup. It helps to remove the extra food from your plate and get it out of your reach before you start eating. Otherwise it is easy to tell yourself while you're eating that you'll leave that last pancake and sausage on the plate, then eat it anyway when everything else is gone. Really, you should be skipping the pancakes and having some oatmeal or cereal instead, but I know how hard it is to start. How about the cakes, puddings, cookies? The minute you get your tray, give those things away! Try to trade for fruits or veggies. People will trade. Stop dumping sugar and salt on everything. Man, so many people I see just start dumping all kinds of stuff in their food before they even taste it. Please, stop that! Just try it and you'll see your tastes and cravings start to change.

Guess what? If I eat a bowl of oatmeal with nothing and you eat one with sugar and butter in it, I will feel as full as you do. The difference is you're adding crap that your body doesn't need, and it shows. Not all food needs to taste like dessert. So many men and women look like triple layer cake, and believe me, I knew it when I did and felt it even more. What are you going to do about it today?

I'm not saying you can never have a junkie snack. Just pick one day for one snack. I usually have something on movie night. I don't go overboard either. When you start tracking what you eat and eating healthy foods, your body will start to crave those foods and excess sugar will taste overwhelming. Sugars from fruit will actually taste better than sugar from cake and ice cream.

If you have no problem cutting things out, count yourself fortunate. Actually, you may be surprised how many people seem to have no trouble cutting unnecessary crap out of their diets. But no matter which category you are in, you can make your diet work for you and your goals.

Starting a Food Journal

Monitoring your progress is critical, and just as you created a fitness journal, you will also use a food journal. Using one journal for both food and fitness is fine. Organize it in whatever way works best for you, either in two separate sections or recording food and fitness charts and emotions every day. The food journal will help you gain a concrete sense of the types and amount of food you have been consuming, the next step is to make a meal chart that will set you up to—depending on your goals—lose weight or just eat in a more healthy way to fuel a more fit body.

Creating Meal Charts

As I said earlier, we will be using charts to plan and track not only your workouts but your diets. These will go in your journal that connects food, exercise and your emotional health and progress. So, what is a meal chart and why make one? A meal or food chart is a record of all that you eat in a day, week, etc. It serves four purposes:

- To monitor the types of food you're eating. At the end of the week you can look it over and see where you need to improve the next week.
- To keep your intake in your face and encourage yourself. Filling out this chart after every meal will keep your goals for your new lifestyle in constant action.
- To hold yourself accountable and stay on the health wagon. If you have a slip up, it's in front of you, so you know you need to work harder.
- To reflect on your progress, learn from mistakes and work through emotions related to food.

Try copying the example on Page Seventy-One, either by hand or with a copy machine if you have access to one. It gives you space for five meals and an option of a small snack if you get really hungry at night.

Shortly I will explain more about what foods to eat, but as far as what you drink, you need to track your water, drinking it all day long. I don't include coffee or tea either (by the way, try to cut down on the sugar and cream you put in both). When I did drink coffee, I used non-fat powdered milk and minimal amounts of sugar. Remember, in here you need to improvise. I tracked two percent milk and real fruit juice. Stop drinking Kool-Aid, which is made of dye and sugar, and check how much sugar is in the juice you are drinking. You don't need it!

Now, what should you eat? The commissary—I know, it's rough. In the back of the book I provide examples of food guidelines I came up with to reach my own goals. Here is a rundown of what is often available that I think is okay: tuna, salmon, mackerel, chicken breast, plain beans, brown rice, wheat bread, bag milk, low sugar cereals, plain oatmeal, grits/cream of wheat, dried fruit, nuts (unsalted if possible—I actually rinse the salt off salted nuts), Carnation instant breakfast or whatever equivalent your commissary offers, protein shakes, low sugar/low fat granola, granola bars. You can find more in the food guidelines at the end.

Now for the condiments: watch it with the sodium. If you can, try garlic or onion powder. I used garlic on everything. Use what you have available on commissary. As far as I know, most places sell garlic, onion, black pepper, mustard and hot sauce. Hot sauce is fine in moderation, but don't dump the whole bottle on your food! Spicy food can speed your metabolism for a short period afterward. Read the labels. There is added sugar and sodium almost everywhere, so you cannot use condiments indiscriminately for flavor.

Even with the guidelines and plans, people still have questions when faced with a food choice. What is ok? Is this? Is that? How do I really know? Use your head. In general, if it is high in fats, sodium, and sugars (especially if it's processed), don't eat it!

I'm not a huge calorie counter, but I do estimate my daily intake. I know it's hard to do in prison, but you can estimate it by reading labels or checking the library and asking around for resources. There may be a calorie counting book available. You may also have one mailed to you.

Below are calories I found on the labels of things I purchased or looked up in magazines. Of course, this will vary by the product and sugar content. You likely have more information available to you now than I did as labeling has changed, so understand this is a rough estimate. Not everything out there is accurate, labels can mislead and nutritionists don't always agree on everything. But again in the situation in which you find yourself right now, just do your best. The effort will pay off.

MEAL	MONDAY	TUESDAY	WEDNESDAY	THURSDAY	FRIDAY	SATURDAY	SUNDAY
BREAKFAST							
SNACK							
LUCNH							
SNACK							
DINNER							

Reference Food Log

Sample Calorie Count (Estimates)	
Piece of fruit	100 calories
Pack of commissary chicken	100 calories
Cup of skim milk	80 calories
Cup of cereal	100-200 calories
Pack of oatmeal	150 calories
1/2 c cook rice	150 calories
Slice of bread	100 calories

As I said, I'm not a huge calorie counter, but from the beginning of my weight loss efforts I tried to be mindful of my meals. Plus, especially for people who like to be in control by organizing, planning and recording, calorie counting can be one way to keep you on track. Even if you don't like to do all that, if you have no idea how many calories you are consuming you should try it until you have a better sense of what you take in every day.

Now, how many calories should you get per day if you are exercising? It depends on your weight and level of activity and other individual factors. In general, recommendations range from 1,800 to 2,400 for adult women depending on your age and activity level. Even if you don't know exactly how many calories you expend per day, if you are trying to lose weight I recommend totaling your calorie intake per day in a typical week before you begin, then dropping a few hundred calories from that while upping your exercise, again, depending on how far you want to go. Most of the machines now at gyms will allow you to input your weight and age and use it to roughly calculate calories burned for that workout period. "And no, you can't multiply that by twenty-four hours in a day because of course, nobody burns as many calories working out as they do during the regular day!"

It's hard to follow everything by the book when you're behind bars, but you can consistently listen to your body and use your head. I've designed this plan from personal experience. I know it works, but you may need to make small adjustments to create what works best for you. If you prefer to count calories, do it! If you prefer to plan your meals sensibly and just wing it, that's how I started. But if you have no sense of what is in your food, I suggest reading the labels carefully to at least estimate calorie intake at the beginning and learn which foods are best and which you can avoid.

So how can you begin? After every meal, jot down what you just had. Keep a constant eye on what you're putting in your body so you can always make improvements.

What did you eat last week? Let's say you only had three bad meals all week. So the next week, try to have one bad snack, and eat well the rest of the week. Try to avoid people who sit in little groups in front of the TV and eat snacks for hours on end. Look at your food chart and remind yourself what you're trying to accomplish while you're here. Getting fat and lazy is not it! I suggest staying more to yourself anyway, unless you truly have found a healthy friendship in which you support each other positively. Staying focused and to yourself can have benefits in this environment, though, because unfortunately, many people here don't want to see you better yourself. They will try to get you to eat badly. They might not have the heart and drive to do what you're trying to do. What better way to make themselves feel better than to pull you down?

"Who cares?" they might say. "It's just a cookie." Yeah, who cares, it's just a gram! Let's get real. We're trying to accomplish a goal, which requires focus and the use of a journal and charts to track progress. This is how you live it. You have to put this first, before the card games, TV show, phone call, or whatever.

Ok, now pick a day of the week. Friday was ideal for me. If that's the day you pick, every Friday go over your food chart for the past week. Get an idea of what you are putting in your body. Are you eating all five meals? Did you eat too much crap? What can you do next week to make sure you do better? Make sure you are eating enough. Do not skip meals. We need to get your metabolism working at its best.

If you had chips Monday, cake Wednesday, and cookies Thursday, that's too much crap! Remember, you're picking just one day to have a junk food snack. This does not make it a junk food binge day—just one snack. As I mentioned earlier, we had movie day and commissary day on Wednesday, so every Wednesday I allowed myself a treat. Now, I personally don't even have the desire to do this every week. On some days I just do not want the sugar because it makes me feel crappy.

Again, let's say you picked Friday as your review day. Compare your old charts showing what you did before with your new chart representing healthier eating. See if you ate all of your meals. Did you eat halfway decent food? Did you try to balance meals? Below is an example from my own tracking process of a decent week of eating, followed by a bad week. Also, I will provide a food chart that I did for myself in Wyatt, the last facility I was in.

Here is an example of a good week I recorded in a food journal when I was locked up.

MEAL	MONDAY	TUESDAY	WEDNESDAY	THURSDAY	FRIDAY	SATURDAY	SUNDAY
MEAL 1	Cream of wheat, apple	Cereal with 1% milk, orange juice	Scrambled eggs on wheat toast, apple	2 pancakes with syrup, banana	2 boiled egg whites, sausage wht. toast, OJ	2 french toast with syrup, orange juice	Oatmeal, apple juice
MEAL 2	Peanut butter on wheat bread	Oatmeal and raisins	1/2 pack chicken, Honey mustard on wheat	Cereal with nonfat milk	Cereal with nonfat milk	Carnation shake	Granola with 2% milk
MEAL 3	Chili, rice, beans & carrots	2 pieces of cheese pizza, salad with Italian dressing	Cheeseburger with lettuce, tomato & cole slaw	Tuna salad on wheat with lettuce, tomato & apple	2 hot dogs on wheat, apple	Ham & cheese on wheat, potato salad, carrots	Caesar salad with chicken
MEAL 4	Cereal with nonfat milk, orange	Carnations instant breakfast, banana	Oatmeal & spoonful of peanut butter	Granola, mixed nuts & raisins	Chicken & beans with hot sauce & garlic	Oatmeal, apple	Peanut butter and honey on wheat toast
MEAL 5	Chicken, potato & green beans	Beef stir fry over rice, mixed veggies	Baked chicken pasta with tomato sauce & broccoli	Spaghetti or Lo Mein, Chicken & mixed veggies	BBQ beef, baked potato & green beans	Lasagna, salad with Italian dressing	Fried chicken, plain mashed potatoes & corn

Adriana Joy Ferns

Here is an example of a bad week for me, which I had noted in a food journal before I lost the weight:

MEAL	MONDAY	TUESDAY	WEDNESDAY	THURSDAY	FRIDAY	SATURDAY	SUNDAY
MEAL 1	Coffee cake with butter, apple juice	Cereal with 1% milk, orange	3 pancakes with butter, bacon, orange juice	Nothing	4 pieces of french toast, 2 sausages, 1% milk	Nothing	Biscuit with jelly & butter
MEAL 2	Nothing	Chips	Cereal with nonfat milk	Peanut butter & jelly crackers	Nothing	Twizzlers, root beer	Cereal with 1% milk, 2 packs of sugar
MEAL 3	3 pieces of pepperoni pizza, Jello-O	Cheese burger with mayo, Potato salad	Chili, rice, beans & Kool-Aid	Tuna salad on white, chips, Kool-Aid	Nothing	Chili mac and cheese, green beans	Nothing
MEAL 4	Oatmeal with 4 packs of sugar	Ramen noodles, Summer sausage	Nothing	macaroni and cheese	Rice, tuna, cheese, butter, Pepsi	Grits with butter sugar	Nothing
MEAL 5	Fish sandwich on mayo on white bread	Chicken stir fry, mixed veggies	Cheesy rice and beans, chicken	Beef & bean burrito with hot sauce, Kool-Aid	Fried chicken, mashed potatoes with gravy, corn	Beef stew with white bread, pudding	Summer sausage, cheese, Ramen noodles

56 • *Fitness to Freedom*

As you can see, throughout the bad week I ate way too much sugar, sodium, and fat, and I skipped meals. It's no wonder I felt like garbage when all I had consumed by the afternoon was Twizzlers and soda. Ugh!

You can also see in the charts that there is a big difference between a proper chart and a bad one. Obviously, if you were home and had access to better food than a prison tends to provide, neither of these would be great. At home you can eat more fruits and veggies, whole grains and lean meats. But behind bars we need to do our best with what we have, so use common sense, read labels and if it's high in fat, sodium and or sugar, don't eat it.

One day when I was still serving my time, a girl said, "You know, summer sausage isn't so bad for you."

I asked her if she had read the label. She proceeded to tell me that she had taken a nutrition class in her last facility and had heard it is not that bad. Who taught that class, Jabba the Hut? People really don't want to give things up sometimes so they make up lame excuses. This is why you need to track your progress and to keep your food chart fresh in your face. This is part of your life now.

In your week's reviews, look at the last week's commissary receipt too. See what you need to cut out. If you don't have it in your space, you will be more successful when hunger strikes.

Next, let's track your weight. If you're lucky enough to be in a facility that calculates body fat, great! What I suggest you do when you weigh yourself is to do it in the morning before you eat and exercise, if possible. If not, that's okay too. Then go have your body fat checked. Write down your weight and your body fat percentage. That's your starting point. Put the date on a calendar, and on the same day next month, do the same thing. If you are doing what you should, you will be pleased with your results. One thing I learned about myself in checking my body fat was that I lose pounds slowly. So when I would get on the scale and see that I had only lost four or five pounds in one month, I was always a little bummed. But I knew I looked and felt better. When they took my body fat, I had lost almost five percent in a month, which was great. I was building muscle, which weighs more than fat and burns more calories. I was okay with that! So don't get discouraged. Doing what I'm suggesting will work if you stick with it. Results that are permanent take time, discipline and dedication. You may have heard before that nothing that's worth anything happens quickly or easily, and it's true. Look at yourself and your situation. For most of us, look at where fast money and the fast life got us. Reaching a positive goal takes hard fucking work! But I know you can do it.

If you do not have access to a body fat calculator and only have a scale, that's all right too. Do yourselves a favor: do not get on the scale every day. Believe me, you will only set yourself up for frustration. Some days and weeks you might be holding more water.

Instead, I suggest you get on the scale once a month. Don't do it when you're all bloated and nasty with PMS or your period. Some people like to get on once every two weeks, which is okay too. Just don't be on it like it's a skateboard. Check your weight, write it down, and track your progress. I was losing one to two pounds per week and felt healthy. If you only lost five pounds and are lifting weights too, don't get discouraged. As I mentioned, I lose weight slowly, but I tend to look like I weigh ten to fifteen pounds less than I do. When I was still trying to lose weight, I weighed 144, but people estimated that I weighed about 120 pounds. At the time, though I was feeling better and liked being complimented, I wasn't satisfied yet. I knew that my body works and feels best when I weigh 130-135, and when I was home for a month, at the gym and eating right, I was 132 pounds and felt like a machine.

That's the point I want you to get to, where your metabolism is a blazing furnace and fat seems to be "melting" off of you! Tracking is an important part of this, and you will be encouraged to keep going when you start to see results. As I know it felt for me, it will feel amazing when people you don't even know well will approach you and say, "Hey, you were thick when you got here, and now you're looking good!" or "Hey, you've lost weight! How did you do that?"

After my initial weight gain in prison, I hated the way I felt physically, mentally and emotionally. As I mentioned, at first, when I was feeling sorry for myself or when I was bored, all I did was eat. If you want to see your progress, be sure to track that, too. What were you eating before you decided to get healthy? What foods and behaviors caused you to gain weight? That's what you know to stay away from in your new life. You need to track it all to see how far you've come, and that will fuel your motivation more than you can see now.

I know some facilities take pictures of inmates for records, and if that's the case for you, there is one more way to see your hard work and dedication in action. Make a before, during and after scrapbook. Include whatever helps you keep an eye on how you're doing.

If you are anything like me, it could be a long haul. The progress I made all started out from changing a little here and there: getting active physically, cutting out certain foods and tracking it all down so I could improve. Don't try to imagine the whole long road just yet, but you can think about and plan for the first month, even the first week if that's what you need.

Knowing what you've been through to get where you are makes it easier to keep going. Take small steps and be aware of each one, and you will get to your end goals. Keep reminding yourself how far you've come. If this is still new and you have not had much time to go far yet, remind yourself of each week's accomplishments and keep moving forward.

As you track your progress in an organized and productive way, keeping yourself accountable and encouraging yourself to keep going when motivation lags, remember that fourth purpose of the food journal in the bullets at the beginning of this chapter. This is also the place for reflecting and working through your emotions so that you can learn from mistakes, deal with setbacks and celebrate accomplishments.

Here you can also reflect on just about anything about your progress. In the food journal section, for example, you could write down how you feel during a diet change. How was your first day/week/month of exercise? When you have cravings, go straight to your journal to write about it and eventually you can learn to crave the pen instead of the food! In other words, rather than going to eat that cake, go to your fitness journal and write about how you're feeling. Think of something you can do rather than eat junk. If you are, in fact, actually hungry, write it down: "I am craving junk but I ate an apple. Two points for me!" If you're keeping track of how you feel and what you're doing, you are in control, and you need to learn control. Many of you might actually be control freaks because you have no self-control. I'm not saying everyone has control issues, but I'm sure you know who you are.

If you're a control freak (ok even if you're not), having no control over the details of your life right now can make you controlling because you want to have control over something! Ok then, make it your health. Grab a hold of what you do have control of such as what you eat and whether or not you work out. In doing this, not only are you getting in shape, you are helping get through some mental and emotional problems.

Your journal will serve many purposes, and I can't stress enough how important it is to keep it in your face. For example, let's say last month you weighed 240 pounds, with 35 percent body fat. This month you weigh 232 with 31 percent body fat, so you've lost eight pounds and four percent body fat. That's motivation in itself! If you've just started working out and your inner thighs are rubbing and chafing, write it down (and put some Vaseline on them before and after; it will help).

Why write all of this, especially the crappy feelings that are driving cravings and issues? In part, it's so you can see what you went through to get where you are. At points along the way, it will be clear that you don't want to go there again. Who wants to go back to uncomfortable feelings that at the beginning we let rule our lives and choices? This journal should be a priority for you, just like your food chart. Do them together.

I once had a bunkie who in prison went to college, worked, and was in the drug program. She still found an hour every morning to walk. She had a bad hip, too! She was overweight, but she was determined and she began eating right. I witnessed her lose inches, and it began with her getting serious about it. So write down everything you're doing, and include your feelings about it. See where your weaknesses lie and work on them. For the best possible results you should incorporate all of the charts, plans, and habits together and make this lifestyle work for you. Try to have faith in yourself, as the old cliché is true: before anyone else believes in you, you must believe in yourself. If you're not there yet, that's okay too. Get started, keep at it, and see if fitness can deliver that faith in yourself you have been looking for. I believe it can. At the very least it will point you in the right direction.

Here are some questions to answer in your journal every so often:

- How is eating right and exercising this week making you feel?
- Do you notice a change in your attitude? Personality? Goals?
- Who are the people you attract? Has that changed? Does it need to?

Negative people will put you down for what you're trying to do for yourself. If you notice it, write it. Use this journal to change. Get away from those people! Remind yourself again that people who do nothing but complain and criticize will hinder your growth. I've repeated this a few times, but it bears saying again to remind yourself of this whenever you need to. After all, you're not exactly in a place full of people who have things together and are living happy lives. You have to be stronger than people on the outside have to be to overcome that crap, and it can be a daily battle until you're in a stable and better place.

By rereading your journal occasionally you will learn things about yourself that you never realized. Why not have everything written so you can truly see how far you've come? Obviously you'll know it, but the point is not to forget the struggle and the stepping stones. Who knows, you could end up helping someone else with your journal.

When I look back to where I was and where I am now, all I can do is smile. I look and feel healthy, and I worked hard for it. Much of my own journal turned into this book, and now it's time to make yours. So do not give up. You are strong enough to do time. Make that time count for something, and track it all in your journal.

For those of you who feel this is a lot to take in right now, you have charts and plans here for just that reason. They can ground you in something concrete so that you can see progress instead of getting lost in or overwhelmed by the subjectivity of your emotions and weaknesses. In the next chapter are recipes and suggestions for meals. Use these and your imagination to eat right. We must do what we have to do while we are incarcerated. Believe it or not, even in this place, you can still follow the old advice: eat to live. Don't live to eat.

CHAPTER 13

RECIPES THAT WORK BEHIND BARS

Many of you don't know a thing about cooking while incarcerated. That's okay. I didn't either. Maybe you don't have microwave access and only have hot water taps. That's fine. As you know by now, it is about improvising, not giving up or making excuses based on what you don't have. If you have access to low sugar, low-calorie granola or cereal bars, oatmeal, cereal, bag milk, bread (preferably wheat unless you are allergic), peanut butter, etc.—buy it. These are great, easy, small meals. If you have microwave access, life is much easier. Even the rice they sell only needs hot water. Again, if possible, use brown rice rather than white. Most facilities buy user-friendly products that suit your whereabouts. Plain, ready-to-eat foods can be fine as long as you are careful to watch your intake of some of the components of food preservatives, such as sodium, saturated fat, corn syrup and other sugars. The following meals are a few of the things I came up with while I was incarcerated. Revise them as needed and get creative (without adding obstacles to your success, such as more sugar). As I've already said, not everything should taste like dessert, but food can taste good and still be healthy. If you can acquire fruits and veggies, you should add them whenever you can. Use a relatively small coffee cup for measurements unless you have access to real measuring cups.

Nutbutter

-Rinse salt off mixed nuts, crush, add peanut butter and mix.

Use on sandwiches, oatmeal.

Chicken or Tuna Salad

-1 pack of chicken or tuna

Mix mustard, garlic powder, pepper, onion powder, ¼ large pickle

(veggies if available, chop and mix).

Serve on wheat or wrap:

1 hard boiled egg. Honey optional.

Remember, if there are extra veggies or fruits and you're permitted to take and save them, go ahead. Don't do anything to get into trouble. If there are extra veggies or fruits and you're permitted to take them, go ahead. Cooked veggies are usually good until the next day if they are stored in a cool place. You're inmates, people, so I know you're resourceful. I was. There are so many ways to make healthy things to eat if you use your imagination. Now that you have an idea of how to reach your goals, put the plan into action. Your diet log needs to be filled out after every meal. Keep it in your face, on your desk, or in another place you'll see it all the time.

Ugh... Cravings!

I know, what happens when your nice neat plan comes crashing against a big fat food craving? For me and for most of the women I knew in lock-up, the worst time for cravings was at night. Why? Who knows? Boredom? All I can tell you is that if you are hungry at 8:00 pm and you don't go to bed until 10:00 pm, you can have something healthy and small to curb your appetite, such as an apple or a handful of trail mix. One of the girls I was helping used to have a few handfuls of Cheerios. Whatever works for you. Keep yourself occupied on something other than food. Read a book or fitness magazine, or write when you're bored.

I used to have a bunkmate who ate little snacks all day, but they were terrible for her. She was eating chocolate covered pretzels, candy, crackers, hot chocolate, cookies, you name it. Then she'd eat her food and dessert from the tray. I tried to help her and she worked slowly to cut things out, but it was crazy. She used to say she was bored, and maybe that was why she ate all that junk. Maybe she had a sugar addiction too. But that can be broken. One good way to stay away from nighttime snacking is by drinking herbal tea. I love chamomile before bed as it helps me relax. If you're eating because you're fidgety, it can keep your hands occupied. It can also help to fill you up.

When you really start to clean up your eating habits, cravings will diminish. Every time you reach for that cake, those cookies, fried chicken instead of baked, two burgers instead of one, stop and ask yourself what your goals are and whether the choice you are about to make moves you toward or away from them. Instead of staring at that cake having a mental battle with it, think about how good it feels to take one step closer to your goals, and don't look twice at the crap you don't need! Look in the mirror and tell yourself whatever you need to in order to understand that you can and will eat right.

Jumpstart Breakfast

-1/2 pack protein powder or 1 package of Carnation-large spoon

-coffee (cool)

-1/2 cup non-fat milk pack of oatmeal

-1 sweetener mix in large cup (16-20 oz) ice cold water

Peanut Butter & Banana Sandwich/Wrap

-1 banana

-peanut butter

Spread on wheat bread or wrap (warm up wrap first).

Substitute honey if no bananas.

Start small.

    If the changes sound like too much all at once, start small. Everything in life that is built slowly seems to last longer. Understand that this will not happen overnight, and you are not a loser if you cannot suddenly do everything I am suggesting. Don't get discouraged. Start cutting small things out of your diet today. Change your commissary list today. Only buy what you need to eat and don't go when you're hungry, fidgety or ready for a binge. Stop buying all that junk! As I said before, if it's not in front of you, you'll crave it less.

Rainy Day Trail Mix

-any unsalted nuts

-dried or fresh fruit

-granola and/or 1 pack of plain oatmeal

-1 pack chocolate Carnation (optional)

-2 spoons peanut butter-small amount

-lowfat milk mix

Eat with spoon.

*Portion control! meant to be mushy.

Apple Peanut Butter Oatmeal

-1 apple (cut into slices)

-1 pack oatmeal

-1 large spoon peanut butter

-mix and add hot water

Heat and eat.

Salmon or Chicken Patty

-salmon or chicken

-crushed unsalted crackers in bowl

Mix: onion, garlic powder, Adobo (a pre-mixed variety spice), black pepper

In a separate bowl: use tomato sauce, hot sauce combo dip, meat/fish dip in bread crumbs.

Heat and eat.

Honey Mustard Chicken Wrap

-chicken

-mustard

-honey

-black pepper

-veggies if possible

Eat on wrap or wheat bread.

Cashew Chicken & Broccoli

-Rinse salt from a small handful of cashews.

-chicken

-broccoli (from tray)

-brown rice optional

-hot sauce

-1 spoon peanut butter

-onion

-3 packs mustard

Cook and eat.

Veggie or Chicken Bean Dip

-veggies if you can get them

-chicken

-plain beans

-garlic & onion

-season black pepper

Mix and heat. Heat tortillas until crunchy and combine.

Hot sauce optional.

Spicy Fish & Grits

-any fish

-2 spoons pasta sauce, hot sauce, garlic powder, onion powder, pepper, adobo

Heat and eat

CHAPTER 14

STAYING MOTIVATED

Maintaining your health and fitness is not just about the food you eat. In order to maintain fitness over the long haul, making a lifestyle change means sitting down and examining everything you consume, and I don't mean just food. This means looking at everything from your reading and television material to the ideas and attitudes of other people that you let in through conversation and association. Choose all of these things carefully, weeding out any that are holding you back and adding those that support and encourage you.

For example, what do you read? Depending on your financial situation, I recommend subscribing to a health and fitness magazine. Two of my personal favorites are Muscle and Fitness Hers and Fitness Rx for Women. Any reputable fitness or health publication will do. You can use these to learn, add new exercises to your routine, keep your new and healthy lifestyle in your face, feel a part of a community with other people who are doing right by themselves, and simply to remind yourself that everything you do is either taking you toward or away from a specific goal. You could also read books about fitness, diet or the positive effects of exercise—whatever works.

Depending on your facility's resources, maybe the library or book cart has some material. Use your facility. Ask for things, whether it be equipment or reading material. Ask, ask, ask. Also, other inmates can help motivate you. If someone has reading material, borrow it when they are through.

The same is true for television. Shows filled with negative people making bad decisions are bad for your brain-and-heart diet! You may think ugh, reality shows and crap tv are my guilty pleasures! Don't take that away too! Ultimately, of course, it is up to you. But as far as I'm concerned, if it's appealing to the negative parts of my own personality, I'd rather be "ingesting" tv and entertainment that's going to keep me in a good place rather than drag me down to petty drama and addictions to the negative in life. I've had enough of that. Plus, I'd rather be using my free time doing things to better my life, not wasting it watching other people ruin theirs. To this day I do not watch television. I don't have cable. I may watch a movie once a month and can honestly say I'm much happier since I've given it up.

The same is true for people. Choose the people you associate with carefully, as we all know how easy it is to rise or sink to the behaviors around us. But at the same time, you never know how much the women you're locked up with have to offer, so don't be afraid to ask for and offer help. When people asked me for help, it put me on a path to training that I have never regretted. Not only did it help motivate them, it helped me practice for my career. If you see someone working out who really looks serious, ask for help. On the flip side, whatever you are good at (even if you're still finding out what that is), don't wait until you get out to offer it to others. Start now.

If you haven't done so already, sit down and write down all that you "consume," excluding food and including all that you take into your mind and heart every day. What on that list is holding you back? Can you cut it out completely, or would it be wiser to gradually reduce that influence? (If you take a gradual approach, map out a plan so you can see the end date in front of you, when the influence will be gone.) What should you add to the list that provides daily or weekly encouragement toward your goals? As I suggested earlier, is there anything you may need to ask for that you hadn't considered was possible? I had to ask for a lot, mostly for classes to teach, equipment or gym time in exchange for work in the gym, etc. I was surprised at how often the answer was yes. I never would have advanced if I hadn't asked for the things that could help me contribute and stay on track. Ask yourself if the same may be true for you.

When you finish this list, create another: what is it that you offer to others around you, whether through your daily work, your friendships, fitness, whatever? If you can't think of anything, add something you haven't done yet but can (tutoring or training someone else in something you're good at, for example).

After making both lists, commit yourself to acting on each this week. Revisit it one week from today and check off what you have accomplished, adjusting your plan as necessary to challenge yourself and reach your goals. Revisit again in one month, regularly monitoring your progress weekly from there.

As you move forward, write out meal plans, exercise plans, goals, everything. By writing things down you have it in front of you and you are more likely to hold yourself accountable. Don't just say you will do something. Put it in writing and structure your new life, recording your notes in your notebook or journal that will keep you focused and motivated. Copy encouraging quotations from books along with any motivating articles you can reread when you're down.

But I'm in lockdown....guess I should just give up for a while?

Again, no! For whatever reason, you're in lock. As I mentioned earlier, I spent three weeks there myself, and believe me I know exactly how easy it would be to give up for a while and how hard it is to maintain fitness there. If you're anything like me, the last thing most of you might want to do is exercise. You may have a negative thought loop playing over and over in your brain and nothing would feel more natural than to spiral down into feeling sorry for yourself.

I'm sure you know by now what I'm going to stay. Stop! Don't trust those thoughts. For a few minutes, try to trust me (I'm your trainer, remember?). Push through one workout in lock, and use that to get on track to do anything and everything to become healthy and in shape.

I won't kid you. It may take every ounce of motivation you possess to do it. I'm hyper so you may think it would have been easy, but it wasn't. Depression weighs heavily on people, even on the energetic ones. But you can do this. In fact, once I got myself to do the first workout, I knew I could do one every day, and the routine actually made the day go by much faster. You want the day to drag on? Just sit there. Want to get through this and make time hurry up until you're out? Get up and work out. Imagine I am in there with you, encouraging you and waiting for you to get up. Tell yourself to stop whining and move.

The type of facility you're in will determine access to commissary while in lock. If you can buy food for your extra meals, great! If you can't, ration out that tray. Save what you can. I would eat my burger at lunch and save my potato salad or whatever side for my in-between meal. I had to wait two weeks until I had access to commissary time, so I really had to be creative. Even if it's not the healthiest food you've ever seen, you must eat. Do your best not to eat the cakes and cookies. Yes, I know how much harder it is to do in this lock. But if you go for the junk, you'll just feel like shit that you ate it. I used to throw it in the toilet as soon as I got my tray so I wouldn't even be tempted. It may sound extreme, but it works.

Being in lock is such a downer that turning to food is much easier. But you can find other things to do. It's great to read, but there are other things to try if you get bored or tired with that. I used to write. I would write poems, raps and lists. I used to write lists of goals and things I want to do with my life. I tried to get to know myself better through writing. What I found was that it helped me to accomplish my workouts and pass my days with routines and things to look forward to. Here's how I did it: at about 5:15 am I would wake up without an alarm. I just always seemed to wake up ten or fifteen minutes before breakfast. I would eat at 5:30 am. Then I would read some of the Bible, listen to music, and write to friends, my boyfriend, family or whoever I felt like writing to. Whatever your beliefs are spiritually is up to you. I just liked to start my day that way. You can meditate or do whatever works to begin your day positively and calmly. But try something that gets you into a good routine and gives you a purpose.

After about an hour, I would start my workout, which took approximately an hour and a half. See Chapter Fifteen on workouts for getting and staying in shape while in lock. Remember that you can, and should, add or take away reps, exercises and times to best suit your own needs. After I did my workouts I would always stretch for about ten minutes or so. I like to use a lot of yoga poses. I've found that yoga moves helped my back from hurting so much due to the lovely mattresses we were given!

Remember, stretching is just as important in lockdown as it is for your regular routine. I already mentioned that it prevents injury and helps relieve the soreness you might experience the next day. It also helps you look and feel better. In my time as a trainer now, I've noticed that a lot of men I see at the gym don't like to stretch. I'm not sure why, but it's even more important when you're cooped up in a place like lockdown.

After my workout and stretch I would wash up in the sink. Before I was able to get to the commissary I would eat something I had saved from the trays. It was usually 8:30 am or 9:00 am at this point. I had something small and when I got my commissary time, I would have a Carnation instant breakfast with nonfat bag of milk. I would usually read until about 10:30 am - 11:00 am, which is when lunch was served. Before I got commissary time I would save something off the tray for my afternoon snack. After lunch I would usually read and write. At about 1:30 pm I would eat the afternoon snack. Once I got commissary I would have oatmeal that I made with hot water from my sink. I would read after that and at 3:00 pm, Monday to Friday, I was allowed an hour of recreation time (not that they ever gave me a full hour, but instead of groaning at that, I told myself to focus on and use what I had). During that time I would run for about twenty minutes, make a phone call and take a shower. That rec time was the highlight of my day and gave me something to look forward to. After that I would read or write for about thirty minutes and then dinner usually came at about 5:00 pm. After eating I would spend the rest of the night reading or writing. I usually went to bed at 8:30 pm.

Those were my days in segregation, and as long as I had a routine that included a workout and the smartest food plan I could create with what I had, the days actually went by almost quickly. My advice is to finish the workout no matter what. If you don't have time outside, work out in place using your body for weight, run in place, do jumping jacks, whatever. Believe me, most of the time I wanted to stop and just try to sleep. Please, for your own sake, push through and stick with your workout routine. It is worth it. Dark as it feels in lockdown, take the word of someone who has been there. Take care of yourself physically and mentally in this situation and you will come out better and stronger because of it.

My Response to Sore Muscles and Other Complaints

Okay, so you try your workout plan for a week or two and you don't see results. You're sore, and it's hard! My response as your trainer? Blah, blah, blah! First of all, nothing on this earth will give you healthy results in two weeks. Not pills, not starvation, not creams. Get real.

If there were some miracle, wouldn't everyone know about it? The only way, especially while incarcerated, is diet and exercise.

The first few weeks are the worst. Of course you will be sore. I still get sore, and I'm in great shape. When I first got home and joined the gym, and when I came back and went to lock, my calves hurt so badly. The concrete in my room made them sore for over a week. I wasn't used to the hard surfaces. On top of that, the sneakers supplied by incarceration facilities are not athletic shoes. They suck! I had blisters and pain in my feet.

Most places do sell shoes. But before you buy all kinds of crap, buy sneakers. It's so important. If you don't have money, find someone who is leaving to give you a pair. Today as I write this, I still have scars on my feet that are not done healing yet. Crazy, right? The fact of the matter is, I had worked too damn hard to let myself go, so I dealt with the pain. Deal with it! On some days, the girls I worked with in prison complained the whole time. Ok, so do the people outside!

I say, "Too bad!"

And the end of the workout, they say, "I feel good!" It made me feel great that after all of their whining, they were happy with the way they felt.

I know I'm repeating myself here, but with the women I worked with, repetition was important. So again, do you really want this? You are worth it, and no matter what anyone else has told you, you can change. I did a 180, finally feeling honestly good for the first time since I was a little kid. There are so many of you up at pill line taking meds for unnecessary reasons. I hear girls complain how their meds make them feel, make them eat, gain weight, etc. I'm not a doctor, and some of you may need those meds. But as I see it, what does a twenty-two year-old need to be on all of that stuff for? Hell, what does a forty year-old need a lot of those meds for? Until I came to prison, I had never met so many whiners and people with problems that most of them had caused themselves and that could be helped by diet and exercise. There is plenty of research to suggest that healthy eating habits and exercise help to keep people happy, energetic, and just plain positive. We all know there are more than enough negative people in your life. Don't be one of them!

As I mentioned earlier, I was diagnosed with ADHD when I was thirteen and put on a variety of meds on and off until I was nineteen. In addition to all the self-medicating I did, I felt frustrated all the time in school because I couldn't understand the content or stay focused. I had more energy than I knew what to do with. Now, I feel focused and I am able to concentrate. The reason I'm telling you this is because diet and exercise was the main reason for my positive change. I can finally say I like who I am, and that feels terrific after years of confusion and self-destructive behavior. I am happy to say I don't take any medication for my ADHD and I feel great about it.

If you can relate to this, please listen. Do you want to end up back in prison again, back where you are now? I know you don't. Only by changing your life and your habits do you have a fighting chance on the outside. It's hard enough to get out of the system once you're in it. Finding someone to hire you is no easier. If you're healthy and positive, you project that energy onto everyone you come across. You attract positive people and good things will come into your life. Would you hire someone who looks unhappy and miserable? I wouldn't! Step back and look at your life, really. Even if you don't like what you see, look. What kind of person do you want to send back out into the world outside? Start bringing her out of you.

You need to try doing something different. No matter where you're from, what you have or don't have, you can change into the best you. I may sound like some cheesy after-school special or a self-help book, but I'm speaking from 100 percent of real experience. I was so fucked up before I got locked up, I probably should have been dead ten times over. I don't know at what point I "got it" exactly, but I do know that once I saw myself in a full-length mirror after close to a year of eating and lying around, I'd had enough. Maybe it started with vanity, but I wanted to look my best for me. Then it became a full change in life. Now my head feels clear. Sure, I have my good days and bad days as we all do, but I don't get depressed or down like I used to. I'm motivated. There are all these new things I want to try healthy and sober. I want to be involved in everything I can do. I wasted so many years getting high, trying to "get one over," make fast money and have dangerous fun, that now I just want to catch up. I'm actually a little angry with myself for not doing all of this sooner, and I hope someone else might learn from my mistakes.

Now, this is your time to turn things around. Sitting around playing cards, watching TV, listening to gossip…just passing the time will do nothing for your future. This is your time to change. Ask yourself if you really want this, because if you do, you absolutely can do this. There is nothing better than taking back your life. I promise.

CHAPTER 15

WORKOUTS IN DETAIL: BEGINNER TO ADVANCED

Now that you have tried some of the workouts I suggested in earlier chapters, use this chapter to individualize a plan for yourself so that you begin at your own fitness level and advance from there. It will also help you avoid plateaus and boredom as you continue to push yourself in whatever situation you find yourself right now, from county to lockdown. If there are any terms for exercises you don't understand, use the photos and glossary at the end of the book.

Level 1: Prison (about 3 weeks)

I've designed this routine for people with access to a track, machines for cardio, hopefully weights and/or cable machines and medicine balls. There may even be some classes available. Starting and sticking with a routine is difficult for the first two weeks, but you must fight through the soreness and uncomfortable feelings you might experience at the beginning. Don't push so hard that you injure yourself, but don't whine yourself into avoiding a good sweat, either. It gets better and the results will be worth it.

Remember, you cannot turn fat to muscle, but the more muscle you have, the faster your body will burn fat. The way I set this up is to build up your stamina and to turn your body into a healthy machine. If you don't need to lose weight and just want to maintain and tone, refer to the medium/advanced plan. If you are using weights, size depends on your strength. Beginning women should start with less weight. Adjust if your facility does not have the necessary equipment or amenity (e.g. a pool for the below), and see the illustrations for help. Stay on this routine for three weeks.

MONDAY	TUESDAY	WEDNESDAY	THURSDAY	FRIDAY	SATURDAY	SUNDAY

REFERENCE CHART: COPY FOR YOUR OWN PERSONAL USE

MONDAY	TUESDAY	WEDNESDAY	THURSDAY	FRIDAY	SATURDAY	SUNDAY
CARDIO	UPPER BODY	LOWER BODY	CARDIO & ABS	CARDIO	WHOLE BODY	CARDIO & ABS
-Walk track or machines for one hour. Try do one machine for 30 minutes and another for 30 minutes. It fights boredom and utilizes different muscle groups. If you need a slower start, try at least to walk for the hour. *Do 45 minutes to an hour of cardio on cardio days. Stretch	-2 sets of bicep curls -2 sets of 10 triceps kick backs -2 sets of 10 shoulder press -2 sets of 10 chest press -2 sets of 10 reverse Roman chair Repeat -30 minute cardio Stretch	-2 sets of 10 weighted squats -2 sets of 10 lunges -2 sets of 10 step ups -2 sets of 10 calf raises Repeat -30 minute cardio Stretch	-20 crunches -2 sets of 10 leg lifts -20 side crunches Repeat abs Walk 1 hour Stretch	-30 minutes on machine -30 minutes of different machine, or walking Stretch	Use benches if you have them: -Walk 1 lap (track) -20 jumping jacks -10 bench push-up -10 step ups each -20 crunches -20 mountain climbers -Walk 1 lap -20 spidermen -50 count footballs -20 flutter kicks -20 walking lunges -10 tricep dips -Walk 1 lap -20 mountain climbers -25 squats -10 bench push ups -20 side crunches -20 jumping -Walk 1 lap Stretcv	-2 sets of 10 knee tucks -30 second plank -30 second side plank Repeat abs -Walk 1 hour Stretch

REFERENCE CHART: COPY FOR YOUR OWN PERSONAL USE

Level 2 (Four to Six Weeks)

If you are moving up from Level One, congratulations! You have made it through close to a month of exercise. How do you feel? Are you a little sore? If so, that is normal and it will get better. I hope you are starting to feel better about yourself. You have made it over the hump. So keep going. I have already mentioned that you have to push yourself. For instance, if you can jog ¼ of a lap and walk one, do that instead of jogging ¼ of a lap. Don't tell yourself you can't.

When I was building up my endurance to run, one day I was up to three miles and I was feeling good. I told myself, "I'm going for five." And I did it! You can do what you put your heart and mind to. Keep pepping yourself up. You may think the thoughts in your brain sound crazy or feel you are weak if you need to give yourself pep talks all the time. But if it is positive talk that keeps you going, that's fine. Stay on this level for four to six weeks, stepping up your cardio by your second week. Jog that full lap or two if you can. If you are on machines, increase the speed and the resistance. Challenge yourself. You can build your endurance more quickly if you like, but don't overdo it (See my earlier note to obsessives).

To those of you who are starting at this level, that's great, but don't take it too easy on yourself. You have to step up your game at every level, challenging yourself to finish all of your workouts (no cutting corners). If jogging half a lap seems hard, go slowly and push through it. This is your second stage workout, and you can do it! I'll see you in a few weeks at the next level.

LEVEL 2

MONDAY	TUESDAY	WEDNESDAY	THURSDAY	FRIDAY	SATURDAY	SUNDAY
CARDIO	UPPER BODY	LOWER BODY	CARDIO & ABS	CARDIO	WHOLE BODY	CARDIO & ABS
-Walk 1 lap -Walk ½ lap, jog ½ lap Repeat for 30 minutes Walk or use machine for last 30 minutes. Stretch	-3 sets of 10 bicep curls -3 sets of 10 triceps kickbacks -3 sets of 10 shoulder presses -3 sets of 10 reverse Roman chairs Repeat -30 minutes cardio machine Stretch	-3 sets of 10 weighted squats -3 sets of 10 lunges -3 sets of 10 step ups -3 sets of 10 inner thigh weight slides -3 sets of 10 calf raises Repeat -30 minute cardio machine Strretch	Walk 1 hour. Stretch	-50 crunches -30 side crunches -3 sets of 10 leg lifts Repeat abs -walk 1 lap -walk ½ lap, jog ½ lap Repeat for 30 minutes Stretch	-Walk 1 lap -25 jumping jacks -25 spidermen -walking lunges, 10 on each leg -jog ½ track, walk ½ track -20 mountain climbers -15 bench push-ups -10 step ups each leg -10 tricep dips -25 crunches -25 jumping jacks -Walk 1 lap -5 burpees -25 squats -15 bench push ups -20 flutter kicks -Walk ½ lap, jog ½ lap -Walk 4 laps -Walk ½ lap, jog ½ lap Stretch	-30 minutes on one machine -30 minute jog/walk alternating or other machine Stretch

Level 3 (Four to Five Weeks)

Congratulations! You're now on the medium/advanced prison routine. This level is your breakthrough. If in fact you are eating right, you should be looking and feeling much better than you did at the beginning. It's not easy to get here, but if you have been following these routines from start to finish, every time you move up a level it is a huge accomplishment. At this point you're locked into living a fit lifestyle, so feel free to be proud of yourself! Be careful, though. This does not mean you can give yourself room for slack or make an excuse. Unless it is your pre-planned one day off of the week, then no, you can't skip a day! Continue to be disciplined. Skipping days in a row and eating crap will just put you back where you started. It takes time (more than a few months) and dedication to mold your self-control.

Stay with this workout for four to five weeks; then move on to the next one. If you feel you're ready sooner, than by all means move up sooner. Remember, these routines were designed for people who rarely exercise if they do at all, or they are overweight or obese. People in fairly good shape should start at a higher level.

Keep up the good work and I will see you at the next level.

LEVEL 3

MONDAY	TUESDAY	WEDNESDAY	THURSDAY	FRIDAY	SATURDAY	SUNDAY
UPPER BODY	LOWER BODY	LIGHT DAY	CARDIO & ABS	TOTAL BODY CIRCUIT	CARDIO	CARDIO & ABS
-3 sets of bicep curls -3 sets of tricep dips -3 sets of 10 shoulder presses -3 sets of 10 chest presses -3 sets of 10 reverse Roman chairs Repeat 30 minute cardio machine Stretch	-3 sets of 10 weighted squats -3 sets of 10 lunges -3 sets of 10 step ups -3 sets of 10 leg presses -3 sets of 10 calf raises -3 sets of 10 inner thighs Repeat 30 minute cardio machine Stretch	Walk 1 hour Stretch	-100 crunches -50 side crunches -3 sets of 10 knee tucks -60 second plank -30 second side plank -3 sets of 15 flutter kicks Repeat Walk 1 lap, jog 1-2 laps Repeat for one hour Stretch	-Walk 2 laps -75 jumping jacks -50 mountain climbers -2 sets of 10 bench push-ups -10 bench lunges -25 crunches -jog 1 lap -20 tricep dips -15 step ups each leg -20 leg lifts -75 jumping jacks -20 spidermen -10 bicycle crunches -25 squats -10 bench push-ups -10 tricep dips -jog 1 lap, walk 1 lap -5 jumping jacks -5 burpees -20 spidermen -Walk 1 lap Stretch	-30 minute machine -30 minutes of walk 1 lap, jog 1-2 laps Stretch	-3 sets of 10 crunch freezes -3 sets of 10 pass offs -50 side to sides -3 sets of 10 leg lifts -100 crunches -2 sets of 10 toe touches Repeat Cardio: Machines, 30 each, or 60 in 1 Stretch

Level 4 (Four to Six Weeks)

You have been working out for about three months now, and you can do anything in life if you stay dedicated to this healthy lifestyle change. You are already succeeding in something that requires extreme will power and dedication.

For example, you can now run a mile or more straight through. You're lifting more weights and you're losing weight more quickly. At this level, I am putting you to work with the cardio to get your endurance built up and to continue dropping pounds if that's what you want (if not, compensate with calories from the healthy food options I recommended in the chapter on recipes). Changing up your routine is a good way to lose weight more quickly; your body responds to change by burning more calories as the muscles you haven't been using are now being asked to expend energy. You are less likely to hit those plateaus you hear so much about.

Stick with the routines on the next page for four to six weeks. The object here is to get you ready for that next level, which is where who people exercise regularly begin.

Yes, you're on your way! While all bodies are different, if you were overweight you should have dropped a substantial amount of weight from where you started. If you're not losing weight then you may not be eating as well as you can. You should be getting results now that are more noticeable. You have officially become a healthy, active person on the way to having the body you've always wanted (or used to have). Get it, get it back!

MONDAY	TUESDAY	WEDNESDAY	THURSDAY	FRIDAY	SATURDAY	SUNDAY
UPPER BODY	LOWER BODY	LIGHT DAY	CARDIO & ABS	TOTAL BODY CIRCUIT	CARDIO	CARDIO & ABS
-Pull-ups until failure -3 sets of 15 tricep dips -3 sets of 10 shoulder presses -3 sets of 10 chest presses -3 sets of 15 reverse Roman chairs -3 sets of 10 bicep curls --3 sets of 10 tricep kickbacks -3 sets of 10 push-ups -3 sets of 10 barbell raises -3 sets of 15 reverse Roman chair Cardio: -30 minute machine Stretch	-3 sets of 10 weighted squats -3 sets of 10 lunges -3 sets of 10 step ups -3 sets of 10 leg presses -3 sets of 10 calf raises -3 sets of 10 inner thighs plate push Repeat -30 minutes cardio machine Stretch	Walk 1 hour Straetch	-100 crunches -50 side crunches -3 sets of 10 knee tucks -60 second planks -30 second side planks -3 sets of 15 flutter kicks Repeat Walk 1 lap, jog 1-2 laps Repeat for one hour Stretch	-Walk 2 laps -75 jumping jacks -50 mountain climbers -2 sets of 10 bench push-ups -10 bench lunges -25 crunches -jog 1 lap -20 tricep dips -15 step ups each leg -20 leg lifts -75 jumping jacks -20 spidermen -10 bicycle crunches -25 squats -10 bench push-ups -10 tricep dips -Jog 1 lap -Walk 1 lap -75 jumping jacks -5 burpees -20 spidermen -Walk 1 lap Stretch	-30 minute machine -30 minute walk 1 lap, jog 1-2 laps Stretch	-3 sets of 10 crunch freezes -3 sets of 10 pass offs -50 side-to-sides -3 sets of 10 leg lifts -100 crunches -2 sets of 10 toe touches Repeat Cardio: -Machines, 30 each or 60 in 1 Stretch

LEVEL 4

Adriana Joy Ferns • 81

Level 5 (Two to Three Weeks)

This routine is only two weeks long and a little more difficult, but you're ready at this point to handle it! It is here to push you to where athletic people are in their workouts. You are an athlete now, and while there are still many levels to build, you have the stamina and drive to do this now.

I enjoy working out and at this point I hope you do too. I know how hard it was to get here so take a minute to be aware of your accomplishment. Many people who are free don't even have the motivation to do what you did! No one can take that away from you.

MONDAY	TUESDAY	WEDNESDAY	THURSDAY	FRIDAY	SATURDAY	SUNDAY
CARDIO	TOTAL BODY	CARDIO	REPEAT	REPEAT	REPEAT	REST DAY
-Walk 4 laps -Jog for 30 minutes -Cardio machine for remaining time This should last 1 hour Stretch	-Walk 2 laps -100 jumping jacks -50 mountain climbers -20 spidermen -50 crunches -20 bench push-ups -20 step ups each side -jog 1 mile -20 tricep dips -10 bench lunges -10 side dip planks -10 burpees -100 jumping jacks -90 second plank -Jog 1 mile -20 bench push-ups -50 squats -20 leg lifts -Jog 1 mile -Walk ½ mile Stretch	-1 hour on machines Stretch	Tuesday's Workout	Monday's Workout	Tuesday's Workout	Stretch & Yoga

LEVEL 5

Level 6 (About 8 Weeks)

The workout routine you are about to do is that of a person who exercises regularly: you! I'm sure your results say it all. People are probably telling you how great you look. Your self-esteem is better. You are stronger physically and mentally. At this point, you really are past the point of needing my help on the particulars as you are experienced enough to design your own workouts. If there are any words to use to describe how you feel, use them. Express in your fitness journal: where you started, and where you are now…it's intense, right?

I suggest you stay on this for about eight weeks. Jog for thirty to sixty minutes once you are about six weeks into this routine. If you are unable to jog use an alternative machine or walk quickly. Go at your own pace, adding quarter miles, half miles and so on.

The routine you are doing now is a routine I used in Danbury prison. I looked and felt great. I was eating healthy and staying strict with my diet and exercise. It was a wonderful feeling, as once you're here you know that if you've made it this far from the beginning, then you really, truly can do anything you put your mind to. Step back and look at how far you've come. Your whole attitude has changed as well as your body. Of course, don't look back for too long. Keep going forward.

Continue varying your workouts so you do not get into a rut or hit a plateau. Throw your body for a loop every few days, working different muscle groups and trying different cardio methods without losing the ones that really make you sweat, such as running. If you can exercise outside, alternate with the gym machines and free weights. Continue to set new goals for speed and intensity, and watch for injuries such as stress fractures and shin splints (you may recognize the twinge if you are prone to them). If they occur, you'll need to replace high impact exercises such as running with lower impact work of the elliptical until you've healed.

MONDAY	TUESDAY	WEDNESDAY	THURSDAY	FRIDAY	SATURDAY	SUNDAY
UPPER BODY	LOWER BODY	CARDIO & ABS	REPEAT	REPEAT	REPEAT	REST DAY
-3 sets of 10 bicep curls -3 sets of 20 tricep dips -3 sets of 15 push-ups -3 sets of 10 shoulder presses -pull-ups until failure -3 sets of 10 chest presses Repeat 30 minutes cardio Stretch	-3 sets of 10 weighted squats -3 sets of 10 lunges -3 sets of 10 leg presses -3 sets of 10 one-leg dead lifts -3 sets of 15 calf raises -2 sets of 20 inner thigh plate push Repeat 30 minutes cardio Stretch	-2 sets of 75 crunches -50 side crunches -3 sets of 20 knee tucks -90 second plank -15 side dip planks -3 sets of 20 leg raises Repeat Cardio: -Walk 4 laps -Jog 45 minutes -Walk 4 laps Stretch	Mondays Workout	Tuesday's Workout	Wednesday's Workout	Stretch & Yoga

LEVEL 6

Advanced Level 7 (About 4 Weeks)

Remain on this last routine (also a level six) for four weeks, and from here you should begin designing your own, mixing it up with classes, videos, weights and machines. The more you change up, the better your results will be. Feel free to use the workout I made up for myself or those in the back of the book.

Let me explain this workout, which I also did when I was in prison. The days you do three to five reps, use heavier weights for you. You should only be able to do three to five reps until your body can't do another with good form. This is to strengthen your muscles, but you do need to be careful to avoid overstraining your muscles or injuring your back and other muscles. The days you do twenty reps, use lighter weight, or at least lighter than your normal ten rep days from your past workouts. This is how you will build endurance in your muscles.

There is no reason at all you should not be in great shape by now. If you're not, you didn't follow what I've advised consistently! If you ate like crap, then there you go. If you only worked out a few days a week, there's the second reason. If that's the case, do not waste time on shame or negative self-talk. Just correct the problem and move on.

So for those of you who made it to this level of fitness and consistency in working out, I know how. In the worst possible situation, you have made a positive change in yourself. No one can take that from you, and if you can do it in this one part of your life, think of what you can do in others! This is exactly how you can be successful in everything you do. As determined as you were to get in shape, ask yourself where else that applies in your life and the choices ahead of you. Now you have the drive and willpower to take on the world. That's the truth. Congratulations!

MONDAY	TUESDAY	WEDNESDAY	THURSDAY	FRIDAY	SATURDAY	SUNDAY
UPPER BODY	LOWER BODY	CARDIO & ABS	REPEAT	REPEAT	REPEAT	DAY OFF
-3 sets of 5-7 bicep curls	-3 sets of 5-7 weighted squats	-4 sets of 10 crunch freezes	-2 sets of 20 bicep curls	-2 sets of 20 squats	Wednesday's Workout	Stretch & Yoga
-3 sets of 5-7 tricep kickbacks	-3 sets of 5-7 step ups	-2 sets of 50 flutter kicks	-3 sets of 20 triceps dips	-2 sets of 20 lunges		
-3 sets of 5-7 chest press	-3 sets of 5-7 leg presses	-50 side crunches	-2 sets of 20 bench press	-2 sets of 20 leg presses		
-3 sets of 5-7 shoulder press	-3 sets of 5-7 one-leg dead lifts	-2 sets of 75 crunches	-2 sets of 20 shoulder press	-2 sets of 20 inner thigh plate push		
-100 crunches	-3 sets of 5-7 side squats	-20 side plank dips	-2 sets of 20 straight arm raise	-2 sets of 20 step ups		
-3 sets of 10 leg raises (Roman chair)	-90 second plank	-2 sets of 10 jack knives	-pull ups until failure	-2 sets of 20 one-leg dead lifts		
-2 sets of 20 side to sides weighted	-60 second side plank	Repeat -walk 4 laps	-2 sets of 20 push ups	-2 sets of quad machine		
-3 sets of 10 weighted reverse Roman chair	-2 sets of 20 leg raises	-jog for 1 hour or machine for 1 hour	-3 sets of 10 lat pull downs	-2 sets of 20 side squats		
Repeat arms/abs	Repeat legs/abs	Stretch	-3 sets of 20 reverse Roman chair	-2 sets of 25 calf raises		
-30 minute cardio	-30 minute cardio		Repeat -60 minute cardio	Repeat -60 minute cardio		
Stretch	Stretch		Stretch	Stretch		

LEVEL 7

Advanced Workout for use in County/Holding

The workout below is designed to speed up your weight loss and endurance level. This one you can do for six to eight weeks (always add extra laps and reps if you feel able).

MONDAY	TUESDAY	WEDNESDAY
CARDIO	ARMS	LEGS
-Walk 5 laps -Jog 25 laps Do this 5 times in a row, end with walking 5 laps Stretch	-Pull-ups until failure -3 sets of 25 tricep dips -3 sets of 15 push-ups -3 sets of 20 push-offs Arms/Back: -2 sets of 25 reverse Roman chair -60 second superman -3 sets of 20 flutter kicks -90 second plank -60 second side planks Repeat arms Repeat abs/back Cardio: -Walk 5 laps -Jog 10 laps -Walk 5 laps -Jog 25 laps -Walk 5 laps -Jog 25 laps -Walk 5 laps -Jog 10 laps -Walk 5 laps Stretch	-2 sets of 50 squats -pick 2 leg exercises, 2 sets of 15 -2 sets of 15 lunges with back leg elevated -2 sets of 25 calf raises Abs: -100 crunches -35 side crunches -2 sets of 15 reverse crunches Cardio: -Walk 10 laps -Jog 25 laps -Walk 5 laps -Jog 25 laps -Walk 5 laps -Jog 10 laps -Walk 5 laps -Jog 10 laps -Walk 5 laps Stretch

THURSDAY	FRIDAY	SATURDAY	SUNDAY
DAY OFF	TOTAL BODY CIRCUIT	CARDIO	TOTAL BODY CIRCUIT
Stretch & Yoga	-Walk 5 laps -20 push-ups -10 jump squats -50 crunches -jog 10 laps -20 spidermen -100 jumping jacks -25 leg lifts -50 side to sides -10 crunch freezes -jog 10 laps -20 tricep dips -10 walking lunges, each leg -20 push offs -40 calf raises -50 mountain climbers -50 count footballs -20 spidermen -Jog 40 laps -Walk 10 laps Stretch	-Walk 10 laps -Jog 30 laps -Walk 5 laps -Jog 30 laps -Walk 5 laps -Jog 30 laps -Walk 5 laps -Jog 30 laps -Walk 5 laps Jog 10 laps -Walk 5 laps Stretch	-Walk 5 laps -100 jumping jacks -15 burpees -20 spidermen -25 squats -20 push ups -50 crunches -Jog 15 laps -25 side crunches -20 triceps dips -10 jumping lunges each side -50 mountain climbers -100 jumping jacks -Walk 2 laps -15 burpees -50 mountain climbers -25 squats -20 push ups -60 second supermen -Jog 25 laps -walk 10 laps Stretch

Adriana Joy Ferns

Workouts for Segregation and Lockdown

And finally, below is your beginner's segregation/lockdown routine. Follow this routine for about four to six weeks, then move up to the medium level. If you are doing everything you are supposed to do, moving up should be no problem. As always, you should keep it in front of you to follow it through your workout. If you do get recreation time, put aside fifteen minutes or so to try and run/walk a little. I realize this is also your shower and phone time, so I'm not saying to spend all of your time exercising. But being stuck in that little room all day is rough. It feels good to run a little.

No matter what it takes, get through your workouts! I don't care if I am repeating myself. Even as a trainer I have days I need to repeat things to myself. On some days, your workouts may feel like the only thing getting you through the day. Don't neglect them. We all need something to get through the day while in lockdown (and on the outside, whether in transition or in regular old life), and it may as well be good for us.

MONDAY	TUESDAY	WEDNESDAY	THURSDAY	FRIDAY	SATURDAY	SUNDAY
LEGS & ABS	ARMS, ABS & BACK	REPEAT	REST	REPEAT	REPEAT	CARDIO
-2 sets 20 squats -3 sets 10 lunges -3 sets 10 inner thigh -3 sets 10 calf raises Abs: -25 crunches -2 sets 10 leg lifts -15 side leg lifts Repeat legs & abs Cardio: -20 jumping jacks -10 spidermen -100 count jog in place -20 mountain climbers -20 jumping jacks -100 count jog in place Stretch	-3 sets of 5 push-ups -3 sets of 10 tricep dips -2 sets of 5 bunk pull-ups -2 sets of 10 bicep curls Abs/Back: -30 count supermen -10 on each side superman -30 count plank (front) -30 count side planks Repeat arms and abs/back Cardio: -50 count footballs -2 burpees -100 count jog in place -20 jumping jacks -50 count footballs -2 burpees -100 count jog in place -Repeat last 4 Stretch	Monday's Workout	Stretch & Yoga	Monday's Workout	Tuesday's Workout	-50 count footballs -5 burpees -20 jumping jacks -200 count jog in place -20 spidermen -20 jumping jacks -200 count job in place -50 count footballs -5 burpees -20 jumping jacks -200 count jog in place -20 mountain climbers -200 count jog in place Stretch

SEGREGATION & LOCKDOWN

As you can see, I add a few reps and some cardio. This is how you build up your endurance and burn more calories. In turn, you are getting healthier and feeling better. This should not be overwhelming if you have been eating right and doing your routines. Feel free to use different days off than what the chart says (that doesn't mean fewer!) and you can add exercises. For your sake, do not take away any exercises or weight at this point. You should have built up to this level if you're not already at it. If this is too easy, move on to the next level.

If you were new to the fitness world and you have just worked up to this, how do your body and mind feel? Keep up the good work. For this next level in lockdown, do this for six to eight weeks or whatever feels right. As soon as it starts becoming a little too easy, change it up to continue challenging your body. Hopefully you're not in seg/lock too much longer. If you are, stay strong. Look what you're doing for yourself! You're getting better through all of this. You're taking control and changing for the better, regardless of your situation. Great job!

MONDAY	TUESDAY	WEDNESDAY	THURSDAY	FRIDAY	SATURDAY	SUNDAY
CARDIO	ARMS	LEGS	REPEAT	REST	REPEAT	REPEAT
-50 jumping jacks -50 mountain climbers -300 count job in place -5 burpees -20 spidermen -300 count job in place -50 jumping jacks -50 mountain climbers -300 count job in place -5 burpees -20 spidermen -50 jumping jacks -300 count job in place Stretch	-2 sets of 10 push-ups -3 sets of 15 tricep dips -2 sets of 10 bunk pull ups -3 sets of 10 bicep curls Abs/Back: -45 count superman -15 each side supermen -45 count plank -45 count side plank -2 sets of 10 knee tucks -Repeat arms -Repeat Abs/Back Cardio: -50 count footballs -20 spidermen -300 count jog in place -50 jumping jacks -50 mountain climbers -300 count jog in place -50 jumping jacks -300 count jog in place Stretch	-3 sets of 10 lunges -2 sets of 20 inner thighs -2 sets of 20 calf raises Abs: -50 crunches -3 sets of 10 leg lifts -20 side crunches Repeat legs Repeat abs Cardio: -50 jumping jacks -50 mountain climbers -300 count jog in place -5 burpees -20 spidermen -300 count jog in place -50 jumping jacks -5 burpees -300 count jog in place Stretch	Thursday's Workout	Stretch & Yoga	Tuesday's Workout	Wednesday's Workout Add 5 to every exercise

SEGREGATION & LOCKDOWN

Medium and Advanced Workouts in Segregation

Now you're ready to move into medium and advanced levels. If you're starting here, that's great. You're already in decent shape and can now work on ways to be creative in continuing to challenge yourself. If you've worked up to this, that is amazing! Nothing can stop you now. Anyone who can stick with this in your predicament has what it takes to do anything she wants with her life. I am sure of it. Make sure, again, to push through discomfort (not real pain or injury) throughout the whole routine. It is important not to quit. Even if you have to go slowly, that is ok, just keep doing it!

If you do get time in some type of recreation area, try to run. Running can feel great after being in your room twenty-three hours a day. If it is a small area, run in circles. It may sound crazy, but running 50-100 laps in these boxes will make you feel so much better. I ran more than 200 laps in one place I was in seg, and it took about an hour. Yes, it can be boring at times and some days I dreaded running in small circles in a concrete box. But then I allowed myself to zone out. I put my music on and got in a zone. If you have two legs that work (and no medical restrictions that would make running dangerous), I know you can do the same. Even if you don't, work out the parts of your body that you can. I used to think of positive things like what I wanted to do in my future. Give it a try.

You can stay on the routine below for six to eight weeks as well. Again, add things if you'd like. Push yourself as much as you can. I hope you're almost out of seg/lock, but even if you have a while to go, keep your head up. You can do it. Learn from this experience.

MONDAY	TUESDAY	WEDNESDAY	THURSDAY	FRIDAY	SATURDAY	SUNDAY
CARDIO	ARMS	LEGS	CARDIO	REPEAT	REPEAT	REST
-75 jumping jacks -50 mountain climbers -500 count jog in place -20 spidermen -75 jumping jacks -50 mountain climbers -500 count jog in place -20 spidermen -75 jumping jacks -500 count jog in place -50 mountain climbers -500 count jog in place Stretch	-3 sets of 10 push-ups -3 sets of 20 tricep dips -3 sets of 10 bunk pull-ups -2 sets of 10 bicep curls Abs/Back: -60 second count superman -20 each side superman -60 second count plank -45 second count side plank -2 sets of 15 knee tucks Repeat arms, abs/back Cardio: -75 jumping jacks -500 count jog in place -50 mountain climbers -10 burpees -500 count jog in place -75 jumping jacks -500 count jog in place Stretch	-3 sets of 20 squats -4 sets of 10 lunges -2 sets of 20 calf raises -2 sets of 25 inner thighs Abs: -75 crunches -2 sets of 10 reverse crunches -25 side crunches Repeat legs, abs Cardio: -50 count footballs -75 jumping jacks -500 count jog in place -20 spidermen -50 mountain climbers -500 count jog in place -75 jumping jacks -50 count footballs -500 count jog in place Stretch	-75 jumping jacks -50 count footballs -20 spidermen -500 count jog in place -75 jumping jacks -50 mountain climbers -500 count jog in place -20 spidermen -50 count footballs -500 count jog in place -50 mountain climbers -75 jumping jacks Stretch	Tuesday's Workout	Wednesday's Workout	Yoga & Stretch

MEDIUM & ADVANCED - SEGREGATION

At this point you should be feeling great (as great as one can feel in segregation)! You're staying busy, you're losing weight and becoming more fit. Keep relying on your charts and journal. You should be comfortable and familiar with different exercises by now, so you can tweak your routine to your liking. I'm sure there are some people who are not comfortable with all of the exercises I put on your routine. Change them if you'd like but keep doing your routines one step at a time. Stay on the below routine for six to 10 weeks.

Just think, once you get out of this place and are able to buy your own groceries, join a gym, run on a track, a beach, etc., you will be ready to live a healthy life. If you are recovering from addiction as I was, becoming more advanced in your workouts can help with staying sober and focused as well. Do not forget the hard work and effort it took you to get here. Be proud of how much you have achieved and do not let yourself slip back. If it happens, go back and read the chapter on setbacks. If you find these workouts helpful even at your more advanced stage, by all means continue to use them. But mix them with your own designs and routines, adding challenge where it is appropriate to avoid plateaus and boredom.

MONDAY	TUESDAY	WEDNESDAY
LEGS	ARMS	CARDIO
-2 sets of 35 squats -2 sets of 25 lunges -2 sets 30 of calf raises -2 sets of 10 leg dead lifts Abs:LEGS	-4 sets of 10 push-ups -3 sets of 20 tricep dips -4 sets of 10 bunk pull ups -2 sets of 10 chest press -2 sets of 25 bicep curls Abs/Back: -60 count spidermen -25 each side spidermen -supermen with 10 leg lifts -60 second planks -60 second side planks -2 sets of 10 knee tucks Repeat arms Repeat abs/back Cardio: -50 count footballs -100 jumping jacks -700 count jog in place -10 burpees -20 spidermen -700 count jog in place -100 jumping jacks Stretch	-100 jumping jacks -50 mountain climbers -700 count jog in place -100 jumping Stretch

THURSDAY	FRIDAY	SATURDAY	SUNDAY
LEGS	ARMS	CARDIO	REST
-2 sets of 25 inner thighs -2 sets of 25 outer thighs -2 sets of 35 squats -2 sets of 25 lunges -2 sets of 25 donkey kicks Abs: -100 crunches -50 side crunches -2 sets of 15 leg lifts Repeat legs, abs Cadio: -50 mountain climbers -100 jumping jacks -700 count jog in place -20 spidermen -100 jumping jacks -700 count jog in place -50 mountain climbers -20 spidermen -700 count jog in place -100 jumping jacks Stretch	-4 sets of 10 push-ups -2 sets of 20 overhead triceps -4 sets of 10 bunk pull-ups -2 sets of 10 dead arm pushups -2 sets of 25 bicep curls Abs/Back: -3 sets of 10 crunches -2 sets of 10 side plank dips -2 sets of 10 rocking leg crunch -60 count supermen Repeat arms, abs/back Cardio: -100 jumping jacks -700 count jog in place -10 burpees -50 count footballs -700 count jog in place -100 jumping jacks -50 count footballs -10 burpees -700 count jog in place -100 jumping jacks Stretch	-100 jumping jacks -20 spidermen -700 count jog in place -50 mountain climbers -50 count footballs -100 jumping jacks -700 count jog in place -10 burpees -20 spidermen -700 count jog in place -50 mountain climbers -100 jumping jacks -20 spidermen -700 count jog in place -100 jumping jacks Stretch	Yoga & Stretch

PART III
AFTERWORD

NOTES

I am sitting at a local coffee shop in Bristol RI, finishing the first draft of this book. I think back seven or eight years and can't believe I am who and where I am today. I have been a full-time Certified Personal Trainer since January, 2011. This past year I was awarded Trainer of the Year by Total Fitness Gyms and I am proud to say I have helped numerous people to lose weight, come off medications, run races and just improve their quality of life. I have had a great time running benefits and educating children about fitness in school health fairs. This year I am running a boot-camp to get my local community more involved in fitness. I am now an activist in my community for GMO labeling and fighting for America's food supply. I have built a vocation in keeping myself and others healthy. I also run a wellness and exercise program at the Wyatt Detention Facility where I once served my time.

Since writing this book, I have learned even more through more education and experience in personal training and nutrition. When I first wrote this book I was incarcerated and had taught myself through trial and error and whatever resources I could find. Since then my exercise routines have advanced beyond sit-ups/crunches and the like, and my diet has changed. On the outside I eat approximately 90% organic when I can help it. I eat a whole or non-processed food diet.

This book came from the heart after experiencing the worst few years of my life. I'd like to reiterate one more thing for those of you facing setbacks even after trying your hardest to turn things around. As you now know, I have experienced plenty of setbacks as well. As I recounted earlier, when I was on the outside again for the first time, I was ripped out of my life and put right back into prison (the vanilla-extract-in-the-coffee debacle). That second time, I had not tried to break the law or game the system. I believe in owning up to my mistakes as it is the only way to avoid repeating them, but heading off to prison again knowing I had been living an honest life for the first time, knowing I had not been looking for a buzz but having lost my credibility almost sent me into another downward spiral. Many of my friends at the time did not believe me and would not believe my conscience was clear. I was so angry and indignant, and it would have been easy to stay that way, dwelling on it as just one more injustice in a crappy world.

But remember what I said earlier about negativity? In the end, I can't blame them for their reactions. They were only going by the behavior I had shown in the past, which had not been honest. I had given them the lens through which they were viewing my life, and they were only responding to the person I had shown myself to be in the past. It was not their fault that they hadn't seen how I had changed. After all, they had known the old me a lot longer than they'd known the new one. Who knew whether I would revert back to the old when so many people do?

So please, don't waste your time on attitudes and grudges that are keeping you from your own health and fitness, especially if you helped create your negative situation by actions you chose in the past. Now, you can do something real and positive and lasting. You don't have as much time to waste as you think you do, so get to it!

These are not empty words or clichés. I have lived what you are living and I will not sugar-coat reality. On some days, life and sobriety can feel like a constant struggle once you have served time in prison. Not only are we trying to live a changed, healthy lifestyle, but also we will forever carry a stigma. Although my probation ended in 2015, I still carry the eight numbers the Federal Government assigned me for the rest of my life. But that's okay. This whole experience not only saved me; it molded me into a person who loves and excels at what she does.

This story is for you. Not to be skinny, not to be sexy, but to be free (yep, in prison). You are in a place where the world says you have no freedom, and the very air surrounding you reeks with unhealthy negativity. But you absolutely are free to choose where you go from here. The system will not help you, but you can. Use your negative experiences to do something different from now on.

In prison I learned how to be free. I am now from drugs, free from low self-esteem, cigarettes and negative people. I am free to come and go, free to eat when and what I choose, and the list only goes on. I am appreciating all the little things so many take for granted on the outside. I can't tell you how often I hear the cliché that people never change. It is not true. I am living proof that people never stop changing. If you are not yet sure if that is true about yourself, take my word for it until you are proving it to yourself.

I have changed so much I am just getting to know myself. There are plenty of qualities that are the same and that I need to continue working on. The good ones are coming to the surface more often and the negative are habits, which I can choose to break. I still have work to do, but in the years since I went to prison I have had more breakthroughs and learned more than many people do in a lifetime. The work began when I asked myself, "What am I doing? What was I thinking? Who am I really?" Have you asked those questions of yourself yet? What role do health and fitness play in your answers and your life?

Now I know where all those corny self-help books I read were going. As cheesy as they can sound sometimes, I still read them and I can relate. Hey, I even wrote one! They did and do help if you take the message the way it was intended. I pray this book helped and continues to help you as you kick butt (even if that has to start with your butt) at the gym and in your life.

Nobody really knows what you are going through but you. That alone can be your reason. Get healthy, get in shape, and get happy. You can become who want to be. Your higher power did not make a mistake. You might have, but it is not too late to fix it. It is never too late.

APPENDIX

GLOSSARY OF EXERCISES

Burpees: From standing position, bend to floor with hands down, jump feet back so you are in a high plank, and drop all the way down (chest to floor). Push yourself up while jumping to bring your feet to hands, stand up and jump.

Butt Blasters: On hands and knees kick one leg back and up so foot is flat, like you're trying to kick the ceiling.

Calf raises/lifts: Stand on floor or a stable edge. Lift your heels and body upward, pushing with the balls of your feet

Flutter Kicks: On back with hands under butt, kick the legs up and down. Make sure your legs stay straight

High Plank: Same position as above, except on your hands with arms straight

Inner thigh raises/lifts: Lie on side, keeping back leg bent with foot on floor.

Jack knife: On back, flat with arms and legs out, try to reach toes with hands (body should look like a V).

Knee tuck: While hanging, bring knees to chest and then lower them back down to straight legs. This should be a very controlled movement and your body should not be swinging. Or, on floor sit up with hands behind you, extend legs out straight then knees to chest.

Lunge: Step forward and with one leg bend both knees and drop back on the back leg so back knee is about 6 inches from the ground. Chest and head are up. Make sure front knee is not over the front toe.

Mountain climbers: On hands and feet (high plank), bring knee to chest as if you're running.

Plank: Face down on mat on elbows/forearms and toes. Hold position.

Side plank: On elbow or hand, stack feet and hold position.

Push-up: In high plank position lower yourself down where your chest is almost touching the ground. If you are unable to get this low at first you may do it off your knees.

Reverse crunch: Lie flat on back bring legs straight up in the air raising your butt off the floor and lowering slowly to bring legs down straight.

Russian twists: Sit up and cross legs (if able to), put one hand over a fist or use a weight and twist to one side. Tap floor and then twist to the other side.

Tricep dips: On chair or ledge, put arms behind you and legs out straight, or with bent knees, bend elbows and dip down.

Single leg deadlift: Stand straight up and bend forward on one knee, your leg straight but knee active (not locked). Your back leg should be straight as you lean forward with chest and head up. Arms hang or hold weights.

Spiderman: In low plank position keep butt down and bring knee to elbow on alternate sides.

Squat: Stand with legs slightly past shoulder length apart. Sit as if you're hovering over a dirty toilet seat. Keep knees behind toes. Push up through heels.

Supermen: Lie face down and raise arms and legs up at the same time as if you're flying.

APPENDIX

GLOSSARY OF EQUIPMENT

Benches:

Just what they sound like, but some will have arms for bench pressing, some will have none.

Pull-up Bar:

A straight bar on a wall or in an exercise tree to do pull-ups on.

Roman Chair:

Looks like a chair with no seat about 3-4 feet off the ground

Reverse Roman chair:

(Back Extension) There are pads at the bottom where your legs lock in and at the top you rest the front of your thighs (Quads)

Squat Rack:

Usually has movable pins or hooks to hold a barbell for you to do your squats with.

APPENDIX

VISUAL DEMONSTRATION OF EXERCISES

Push-up

Plank

Spiderman

Adriana Joy Ferns

Spiderman

Mountain Climber

Mountain Climber

Squat 1

Squat 2

Lunge 1

Lunge 2

Flutter Kicks 1

Flutter Kicks 2

Jack Knife

Reverse Crunches 1

Reverse Crunches 2

Superman

Modified Push-up 1

Modified Push-up 2

Tricep Dips 1

Tricep Dips 2

Tricep Dips 3

Tricep Dips 4

Butt Blasters

Standing Calf Rises

Burpee 1

Burpee 2

Burpee 3

Burpee 4

REFERENCES

i. Covington, S., & Bloom, B. (2006) Gender-Responsive Treatment and Services in Correctional Settings. In E. Leeder (Ed.) Inside and Out: Women, Prison and Therapy (pp. 9-33) Binghamton, New York: The Haworth Press, Inc.

ii. Data Source: The Prison Index (2003) Page 29.

iii. Council of State Governments. (2005, January 16). Charting the Safe and Successful Return of Prisoners to the Community. Retrieved 2015, from https://csgjusticecenter.org/wp-content/uploads/2013/03/Report-of-the-Reentry-Council.pdf

iv. Scott J. Vander Hart, "Does Prison Substance Abuse Treatment Reduce Recidivism?" Performance Audit Report, Iowa Department of Corrections' Substance Abuse Program (May 25, 2007), http://publications.iowa.gov/5092/1/DOC_Substance_Abuse_Report.pdf

v. Mayo Clinic Staff. (2014, September 5). Water: How much should you drink every day? Retrieved 2015.

ABOUT THE AUTHOR

When she was thirteen, Adriana Ferns was diagnosed with ADHD and began slipping through the cracks of the educational system. She began experimenting with using, selling and transporting drugs, and at the age of twenty-seven she was arrested for possession of more than seventy-five pounds of methamphetamine. In March, 2007, while being held without bail in Newark, New Jersey to await trial, she discovered she was a natural teacher when she became a speaker for the Reality Check Program, where she spoke to at risk children to help them avoid prison. After teaching a young woman from Ghana how to read and write, she knew her life would revolve around teaching.

But she still had no idea what she would teach, or that she would one day become a top personal trainer at a chain of New England gyms. In fact, while she was incarcerated and working on her 500 hours of drug rehabilitation, she would go downhill first. She replaced drugs with food and gained thirty pounds before realizing she was on her way to obesity unless she could find a way to turn things around. As she struggled to figure things out and was transferred from one prison environment to another, she began to see the ways that prison systems for women were limited in allowing incarcerated women to maintain physical health and fitness. Believing that changing this was more important to rehabilitation and positive future life outcomes than leaders of the system seemed to realize, Adriana created her own workout and nutrition routines—first for herself, then for others.

When other inmates saw the results she was achieving for herself, one by one they began coming to her for fitness advice, and her life as a trainer began. She was approved to teach exercise classes to other inmates, who found that her solutions worked for them too, not only for getting and staying fit while incarcerated, but after leaving the prison system.

After serving her time, Adriana became certified by the National Council for Strength and Fitness Personal Training and Nutrition to begin a career in personal training. In 2012 she won the top trainer award in 2012 for the Total Fitness chain of gyms in New England, and as a personal trainer, teacher and speaker, Adriana now spends her time helping others to create emotional and physical health through physical training. She also enjoys volunteering her time talking to inmates at a local detention facility, running benefits to raise money for Save the Bay, teaching at summer programs for children in urban areas and working at a local soup kitchen. She lives in Rhode Island.

Copyright August 25, 2017

TXu 2-057-211

Made in the USA
Columbia, SC
27 July 2024